How We Lived

Everyday Furniture, Fashions and Settings

1880-1940

Peter Swift Seibert

Schiffer Publishing Ltd®

4880 Lower Valley Road, Atglen, PA 19310 USA

Dedication

I dedicate this book to the great women of my life.

To my great-grandmothers Kate Tuck Swift and Laura Jane Harris Barr who, although I never met them, provided a wonderful legacy by passing down some of the images for this volume.

To my grandmother Mary Harris Barr Swift who somehow passed her wonderful sense of Victorian propriety to her grandson.

To my beloved mother, Gladys Jane Swift Seibert, who passed away in March of 2001. This book has been part of the healing process in recovering from this horrible loss.

To my wife Cathie, who probably would have rather had me than this book during the months that it was in preparation. My daughter Jane Swift Seibert for whom this book was written as a legacy not only of her father but also the world of her family.

Finally, and most profoundly, this book is dedicated to my sister, Jeanie Cunningham (nee Susan Swift). Jeanie never knew what it was like to have the life contained in many of these photographs. She has had many homes over the years. Perhaps she can find some solace in these images as well as in the love of her brother.

Peter Swift Seibert, June 2002

Library of Congress Cataloging-in-Publication Data:

Seibert, Peter S.
  How we lived: everyday furniture, fashions and settings, 1880-1940/by Peter Swift Seibert.
    p. cm.
  ISBN 0-7643-1743-1 (pbk.)
  1. Interior decoration—United States—History—19th century. 2. Interior decoration—United States—History—20th century. 3. Decorative arts—United States—History—19th century. 4. Decorative arts—United States—History—20th century. 5. United States—Social life and customs. I. Title: Everyday furniture, fashions and settings, 1880-1940. II. Title.
NK2003.5.S45 2003
973.8'022'2—dc21

                    2002156714

Designed by John P. Cheek
Cover design by Bruce M. Waters
Type set in Tiger Rag LET/Souvenir LtBT

ISBN: 0-7643-1743-1
Printed in China

Published by Schiffer Publishing Ltd.
4880 Lower Valley Road
Atglen, PA 19310
Phone: (610) 593-1777; Fax: (610) 593-2002
E-mail: Info@schifferbooks.com
Please visit our web site catalog at
www.schifferbooks.com
We are always looking for people to write books on new and related subjects. If you have an idea for a book, please contact us at the above address.

This book may be purchased from the publisher.
Include $3.95 for shipping.
Please try your bookstore first.
You may write for a free catalog.

In Europe, Schiffer books are distributed by
Bushwood Books
6 Marksbury Avenue
Kew Gardens
Surrey TW9 4JF England
Phone: 44 (0) 20 8392 8585
Fax: 44 (0) 20 8392 9876
E-mail: Bushwd@aol.com
Free postage in the UK. Europe: air mail at cost.

Contents

Acknowledgments 4

Introduction 5

Chapter 1: The Impact of Photography 7

Chapter 2: Working for a Living 18

Chapter 3: The Stereo Card 35

Chapter 4: The Parlor 48

Chapter 5: Looking Backward 65

Chapter 6: The Arts & Crafts – A Mission in Life 76

Chapter 7: Horsing Around 88

Chapter 8: Relaxation & Leisure 99

Chapter 9: Technology Changes Everything 122

Bibliography 128

Acknowledgements

Many people have helped me in the preparation of this manuscript. First and foremost is Peter Schiffer, who has been my partner in producing books for the Heritage Center Museum during the last five years.

Many dealers in antique photographs have helped in locating images for this book. In particular, I would like to thank Kevin Randolph of San Francisco, who aided me in finding so many of the key photographs. His ability to locate a myriad of such images was invaluable and I recommend him to any student seeking historic photographs.

Introduction

We who are living at the beginning of the twenty-first century must think we are experiencing, as composer Paul Simon wrote, "an age of miracles and wonder." While this may be true, arguably the world of 1900 was on the threshold of even greater changes for mankind. Today, we take much of our high-tech world for granted. Recall that to someone born in 1890, in a horse and carriage world, it was a huge stretch to consider that you could live to see man walk on the moon in 1969. While there have been great changes in science and technology over the course of human existence, the leap from horse travel to space flight must rank as the greatest of them all.

Interestingly, and perhaps because of the parallels with our own time or maybe the perceived differences, there is new-found fascination with the world of 1900. Some of this relates to the millennium celebrations when the world not only looked to the future but also glanced back at the past. The recent public television programs "1900 House" and "Frontier House" provided a particular focal point for those interested in seeing what the world was like at the beginning of the last century. Both the celebrations and the television specials were successful in showing how very difficult those times were, compared to the present. They were not content to glorify the past.

A college professor of mine posed the question, *To what time could we post-post modern humans travel back and find ourselves able to live and function?* An interesting question to play with in your mind as you travel a particularly boring stretch of road. The conclusion that most in the class came to was the world of around 1910. Any earlier and the basic values and mindset of society were too far removed from our own experiences. It is important to remember this conclusion, as you read this book. Try not use modern values in judging those of the past.

Despite this question, there still is a significant part of the American public that looks to a real historic past as being better than the present. This is neither a new nor particularly original phenomena. The ancient Romans copied art from the ancient Greeks. Schoolgirls in the 1790s worked stitched images of Christopher Columbus discovering America in the 1490s. During the Victorian period, in particular with the rise of the modern factory system, writers such as Henry David Thoreau and others dreamed of the earlier agrarian ideals that they perceived as being seminal to America's existence.

In design, we call this the Colonial Revival, although the eighteenth century was not the only period being revived. One can find revivals of nineteenth century classical furniture and even Victorian styles occurring during the early twentieth century. The desire to look backward as we move forward, sometimes romanticizing the past and other times being critical of it, is perhaps the greatest hallmark of American interior and exterior design.

Today, we have newfound fascination with the world that existed at the end of the nineteenth and beginnings of the twentieth centuries. Historic house museums looking at early twentieth century life have been springing to life throughout the United States and Canada. Examples include Craftsman Farms in New Jersey looking at the life of Arts and Crafts designer Gustav Stickley and Historic Fort Steele in British Columbia focusing on daily life in a small Canadian railroad town in the early years of the twentieth century. Books on exterior and interior design for this period have also appeared in abundance. Robert Winter and Alexander Vertikoff's *American Bungalow Style*, Malcolm Haslam's *In the Nouveau Style* and Carla Lind's *The Wright Style*, among many, look at particular aspects of late nineteenth and early twentieth century design. Some are designed as guides for collectors and decorators, while others provide more traditional academic discussions of styles and movements.

Of all the literature written about this important time, none stands out more strongly than William Seale's *The Tasteful Interlude*, copyrighted in 1981 by the American Association for State and Local History. As a young museum professional, this book was my bible when it came to understanding Victorian design and style. Seale pioneered the use of original historic photographs to interpret American interior design from the Civil War to the outbreak of World War I. Using only documented and dated interiors, he clearly and accurately defined the changes that occurred in late Victorian America. Even now, after twenty years, his essays and captions remain fresh and informative.

While there are abundant pre-1900 photographs, the only drawback of Seale's book is that his images from the twentieth century are lacking. Only a few Arts and Crafts rooms are shown as examples. Similarly, in his quest for documented interiors, Seale naturally utilized spaces that belonged to the affluent and well known. The home of James Ross Todd, a relative of President Abraham Lincoln, is such an example. It is quite understandable that homes of the rich and famous are more likely to be documented than snapshots of middle class homes that were never captioned. The absence of these images makes this book a next step.

It has been my goal here to show a broad range of images from the late nineteenth and early twentieth centuries. Instead of showing strictly affluent interiors, the images in this book predominantly show middle class spaces. In addition, more than strictly interior spaces are shown. Exteriors, public and private gardens, amusements, carriages, and more are used to illustrate daily life during the period from 1880 to about 1940.

This span encompasses the tremendous artistic, political, and social changes that occurred. A family might be posed with their favorite horse and carriage in front of a house during the 1890s, and forty years later the same group–albeit much older–appear with their first car. Whereas the parlor table was the focal point of Victorian interior spaces, the console radio took this place by the 1930s.

While change is an important part of these pictures, there is also an air of stability and tradition in most of the rooms. Unlike spaces created by interior decorator or architect, where designs flow together in harmony, the spaces illustrated here reflect many styles over many years and human experiences. To understand this, one need only look at the furniture that was popular in the 1820s that was then banned to the chicken coop by the 1860s, moved to the children's bedroom in the 1890s, and then returned to the parlor–newly stripped of its original finish–in the 1930s. Similarly, households with modern furniture would frequently be decorated with objects to create a Victorian "art grouping." The shelf with lambrequin, pitcher with peacock feathers, and balanced curios are a design mode that lasts to the present. Today it might include the macramé cover, bust of Elvis, and air plant.

As you study these photographs–and I hope you spend far more time with the photographs than the text– imagine the changes going on around these subjects; the automobile, airplane flight, and so much more were only steps away.

Chapter 1
The Impact of Photography

One can easily argue that the invention of the camera and the popularization of photography were among the most revolutionary changes to domestic life in the history of man. From Presidents to African tribal chiefs, everyone and everything could be, and often was, the subject of a photographer. The exact realism of a photograph certainly changed the history of art as color and form came to replace the realism of earlier painting. The camera could do it better and so the artist sought out new forms of self-expression. Thus we have the rise of abstractionism in painting.

The Artist and the Photographer

The relationship between the painter and the photographer was one of both love and hate. For the Impressionists, photography represented the opportunity to explore color and form in new ways. It also influenced painters such as Mary Cassatt who used the clipped framing of the photographic image as a tool in the positioning of subjects. For traditional landscape painters, photography was the death knell of their art. The camera could, and did, capture a more realistic landscape. Further, the inexpensive cost of photographic reproductions meant that anyone could own an image of Yosemite or the Grand Canyon. As a result, landscape painting lost its popularity.

Looking East from Grand View Point from *View of Grand Canyon Arizona*. This colored photographic print was published in the early twentieth century for an audience fascinated by imagery of the American west. Published by John G. Verkamp and the Chicago Photogravure Company, circa 1910.

For the portrait painter, however, the camera proved to be most troublesome. In the 1850's, when popular photography was in its infancy, photographic portraits were expensive items obtained in big cities by the affluent. Within twenty years, the technology had so improved that anyone, and everyone, could have a set of photographs taken of their family. For the portraitist, especially those working in smaller towns and rural locations, this was the end of their profession. In the large cities, portraitists continued–and in some cases flourished–as they provided their services to the rich.

Elsewhere, the portrait painter had to learn a new set of skills. Colorizing photographs became one of the chief occupations for portraitists. The gentleman shown here is wearing the regalia of a member of the Independent Order of Odd Fellows–a men's fraternal and benevolent society particularly popular in the nineteenth century. Taken as a black and white photograph around 1890, it was then colored by an unidentified artist.

To our modern eyes, the image is strange and disturbing. The attention to the color in the background and regalia is not matched in that of the face or hands. Facial pigments have been applied but the features remain weak and almost hidden. Adding embellishment to faces, beyond adding skin color, was an extremely difficult task. The result is that most faces were not painted to allow the realism of the photographic image to shine through.

This gentleman is wearing the regalia of a member of the Independent Order of Odd Fellow–a men's fraternal and benevolent society. The sash and apron, along with the book, table covering and background have all been hand-colored. Only the hands and face have been left uncolored. Housed in a faux marble painted wooden frame, this is the late nineteenth century equivalent of the eighteenth century oil portrait. Signed indistinctly by the colorist and unknown photographer, circa 1880-90.

From Studio to Candid Photograph

The earliest images were studio photographs made popular in the small *carte de visita* format or the larger cabinet cards. Taken in professional studios, often with skylights built in to provide the maximum amount of light, these images were the standard product of most commercial photographers. My great-great grandfather, Josiah Swift, had his photograph taken in the late 1860's or early 1870's. Looking at his image and realizing that he and I are of the same age–in our mid thirties–it is easy to see how the rugged life of the nineteenth century world could take a toll on a person. Carefully posed in a studio with a film that required a long exposure time, Josiah is shown as a stern and unsmiling figure. To understand why subjects rarely smiled in nineteenth century photographs, try the experiment of sitting perfectly still and holding a smile for thirty or sixty seconds.

Josiah Swift was born in 1826 near Meadville in Crawford County, Pennsylvania. This image was taken in the early 1860's when he was working as a drayman in the oil boomtown of Titusville. It is typical of the formal studio portrait that rural and urban photographers produced. Unknown photographer, circa 1860-70.

The August 1919 wedding luncheon of Josiah Swift's granddaughter–Gladys Elinor Swift–to her new husband Louis Gause was witnessed by a large group of family and friends. The dining room, probably at a hotel, was decorated with flowers and paper ornaments to commemorate the occasion. Sadly, the new Mrs. Gause died of an unexpected illness just a year later. Unknown photographer.

By the time of Josiah's grand daughter's wedding in August of 1919, a remarkable change had occurred in photography. First and foremost was the use of better films, lenses and developing processes that increased the size and tonal qualities of the image. Second, and probably attributable to the popularization of photography as a past time, was the relaxation of poses. In looking at this image of the wedding party, one does question whether anyone other than the bride is having a good time. Some people look bored, others puzzled while there is a bit of defensive angst in the man on the far right (the bride's brother who disapproved of the wedding of his only sister to a man who turned out to be a ner'do well). The point is that emotion can be far more easily read in this image than the more formal studio portrait of Josiah taken fifty years before.

Advertisements by Sears Roebuck and dozens of other retail businesses for cameras and supplies during the late nineteenth century was, quite arguably, the biggest change to have affected photography. The development of the portable camera and flash attachment, along with inexpensive commercial developing, meant that anyone could become a photographer. As a result, the subject matter also changed dramatically. Illustrated in the next series of images are photographs taken probably by a college age student at Yale. Housed in a scrapbook, regrettably without any names, they show the upscale lodgings for the student as well as various trips taken overseas and to the western United States. In these images, taken for very personal use, any hint of the formal studio image disappears rapidly. The lecherous man leering at the demure girl is just one example of how every topic and person became fair game for the amateur photographer.

These three images are taken from an anonymously compiled scrapbook belonging to a student at Yale University. One can only imagine the story behind the scene of the leering man and the demure young lady. Another interesting contrast is the formal attire worn by the ladies at the dude ranch in Wyoming. Unknown amateur photographer, circa 1900-10.

Another example of the impact of the candid photograph is in exterior imagery. Historically only important buildings were the subject of the professional photographer. Again, with the popularity of the camera, personally important buildings also were photographed. Such an interest in objects of personal–as opposed to national–pride was an important aspect of late nineteenth century photography. Whether a photograph of a gas driller's shack in New York or a large Midwestern home, people wanted a visual testament to their prosperity.

This *carte de visite* size photograph is believed to date from the 1870's or 1880's and shows one of the buildings on the grounds of the Pennsylvania State Capitol. Although the location of this building is not certain, it is typical of a whole genre of photographs taken of government and religious buildings that were popular in the 1870's and 1880's. Unknown photographer, circa 1880.

This is a print from a glass plate negative taken by an unknown amateur photographer who apparently grew up in New York but then moved to Washington, DC. The paper label on the negative sleeve describes this as "Brooklyn P.S. 15. E's first school." Unknown photographer, circa 1920-30, from an original glass plate negative.

This image shows a shack used by a natural gas driller in New York state during the late nineteenth century. The text on the reverse reads: "Grandpa Brands shanty, 2 miles from Kanes Halm in woods. Milton Perry Holly on Porch. Worked for United Natural Gas Company taking pressure of wells in the surrounding woods and countryside." Although to our eye, this seems like an unlikely subject for a photograph, it was someone's home and therefore a source of pride. Unknown photographer, circa 1890.

Such interest in memory also gave rise to another aspect of nineteenth century photography–the memorial card. To modern viewers, images of dead people and mourning corners in homes seem macabre and bizarre. Who would want to remember a loved one in the throes of death? Today, we celebrate life rather than the act of passing. For the late nineteenth and early twentieth century world, coming to grips with death through photographic imagery was an important part of life. The cabinet card illustrated here is an example of a mourning image. While perhaps staged for the camera, specific areas set aside for mourning were an important part of daily life in this period. Here lilies, roses and greenery flank a photograph of the deceased subject. Again, the impact of photography was such that a suitable memorial could be using a photograph as the centerpiece of such a scene. And, so everyone in the family would be able to share in the mourning, the scene was photographed and copies distributed. Death, like a home or a college dorm room, was an important subject to be memorialized in a photograph.

Images of the exteriors of homes were, and still remain, a popular subject for formal photographs. This image is of a typical mid-western farmhouse. Notice, however, the lack of ornamental plantings around the exterior. This was probably taken just after the house was constructed and the family had not yet begun to think about plantings. Another possibility is an aesthetic, still found among the Pennsylvania Germans that eschewed decorative plantings as dirty and impractical. The image is titled on the reverse "Home of E.G. Uuling, Salina Kansas. Visited by Mr. and Mrs. Reuben Hoff and son Chas. E. 1887." Unknown photographer.

The Exotic and Unusual

When Hayden visited Yellowstone in the late nineteenth century to photograph its majestic beauty, he traveled with a wagon load of photographic equipment. His imagery, copied and marketed extensively throughout the east, brought the beauty of this area into the popular consciousness with the result that it was created as our first National Park in March of 1872.

The quest for the exotic and unusual was one that the American public craved in the late nineteenth and early twentieth centuries. The magic lantern–a precursor of today's slide projector system–was one of the many ways of showing exotic scenes to the public. Sometimes in black and white, and other times hand colored, these images brought distant places into parlors in Peoria and Boston. The American Indian was also another subject for the commercial and amateur photographer. Shown here is a view somewhere in Colorado or New Mexico of two Indians carrying bundles of sage on their backs. Taken by W.H. Jackson and Co., the firm promoted themselves as taking "Photographs of Rock Mountain Scenery."

Exotic scenes did not have to be taken far away either. Unusual features of nature, such as a tugboat caught in ice, were also popular for amateurs and commercial photographers. Changes in film technology and equipment allowed such scenes to be photographed in the 1910s whereas earlier it would have been impossible.

The rites associated with death and mourning played an important role in daily life during the nineteenth century. In particular, many east European immigrants had photographs made of corpses or of the mourning flowers that were then to be given to family members as a remembrance. This example is particularly interesting in that it is a photograph of another photograph. The photo in the image is decorated with lilies that were among the most popular of mourning flowers. Marked on the side and reverse "Boyd and Weller, Lafayette IA," circa 1890.

YELLOWSTONE NATIONAL PARK.
PUBLISHED BY F. JAY HAYNES, FARGO, D. T.

YELLOWSTONE NATIONAL PARK.
PUBLISHED BY F. JAY HAYNES, FARGO, D. T.

European and American VIEWS.

European and American VIEWS.

305a
Yellowstone Park.

These scenes, all dating from the late nineteenth century, show various views around Yellowstone Park. F. Jay Haynes popularly marketed a series of photographs of the park to audiences throughout the United States. The stereocards are interesting contrasts because while showing the beauty of the landscape on one hand, they also show man and his influences on the park. The view of obsidian cliffs has a horse and carriage on the road while the hotel scene, with a cut tree in the foreground and buildings in the back, is far more obvious in its depiction of the intrusion of man into the landscape. Photo titles: *Great Falls of the Yellowstone* taken by F. Jay Haynes, St. Paul Minnesota, circa 1890; *Yellowstone Park* from the O.K. Grocery and Supply House. "One of these Views given with one pound of coffee or one-half pound of tea. Twenty-five views will entitle you to one Stereoscope. Dan Riegel." Circa 1890; *Obsidian Cliffs, Yellowstone National Park.* Published by F. Jay Haynes, Fargo, D.T. circa 1890.

Great Falls of the Yellowstone.

4202—Great Falls of the Yellowstone.

Magic lantern slide of a bridge. Unknown company, circa 1890.

This scene of two Indians carrying brush was probably taken in either southwestern Colorado or northern New Mexico. Dating from the late 1800's, the image was produced for parlor use throughout the United States. Credited on the reverse "W.H. Jackson and Co. Photographs of Rocky Mountain Scenery, Denver, Colo."

The World Made Smaller

Photography was not strictly an American phenomena. Rather, the impact of the camera swept the world in wave after wave. Illustrated here are a series of non-American photographs showing candid and studio imagery taken from around the world. All were collected in the United States. Some may have been mailed here while others were no doubt brought by immigrants remembering the life in the country they left. As keepsakes and memories, they are undoubtedly among the most personal possessions that one can have.

A Moment in Time

In looking at the images in this book, I continue to be humbled at the lives that are captured here. Sooner or later, all of us will "thin out" and be reduced to memories and images. The lives of these folks are chronicled in the images on these pages. Look upon them as the sole visual reminders of their existence.

This print was made from an original glass plate negative taken by an amateur photographer during the early twentieth century. Dramatic scenes such as this were popular for both amateur and professional photographers. Unknown photographer.

This image was acquired on the west coast of the United States so it is difficult to know whether the scene was in Asia or North America. Immigrant Chinese workers came to the Pacific coast in large numbers during the nineteenth and twentieth centuries to work on the railroad. Establishing their own enclaves in towns like San Francisco, they continue to carry on a rich language, food and clothing tradition. Unknown photographer, circa 1910.

This scene is probably from somewhere in present-day Germany or Austria. The young man is wearing the military uniform of someone from the Central Powers of the World War One period. Other than recognizing the uniform, little else in this room can be used to distinguish the scene from America or Europe. Unknown photographer, circa 1916.

Chapter 2
Working for a Living

Like today, workers in the late nineteenth and early twentieth centuries often identified themselves by their position within a company or shop. The late nineteenth century was a time period still in transition between small individual shops and large offices and businesses. Similarly, there was a change in the location of shops. In this period, there were both small retail establishments attached to homes and large stores established in separate buildings away from the residence of the shopkeeper.

P. & R. FREIGHT OFFICE EMPLOYES
Harrisburg, Pa., September 25, 1908
JOS. S. KLINEDINST, Agent
HOWARD MENGEL, Chief Clerk
"Should Auld Acquaintance Be Forgot."

Assembled here are the managers and workers at the Harrisburg office of the Pennsylvania and Reading Railroad Freight Office. Unknown photographer, dated September 25, 1908.

Today, the idea of working at home is regarded as the ultimate luxury. In the nineteenth and early twentieth centuries, many people worked at home. In small towns, such as Claysburg, Pennsylvania where this image was taken, business owners would often erect small shops adjacent to their homes. Mr. Black was obviously a successful businessman to have erected the fine four square style house as well as the adjacent tobacco and ice cream shop. Today's modern sensibilities would not permit the open mixing of two such vices—tobacco and sugar. Marked "Claysburg Novelty Company," circa 1910.

Office spaces were also changing dramatically. During much of the nineteenth century, businessmen would often keep offices in portions of their homes. By century's end, the office building was firmly entrenched as the norm for most businessmen. Note the differences in the images shown here of an intimate home office containing oil paintings and other family possessions and an office in an office building. It too has a number of personal possessions although the overall feeling is very different than the home office.

This intimate snapshot reveals much about home offices of the early twentieth century. Older homes fitted for gas fixtures did not have an abundance of floor outlets for electricity. The result is that many rooms, like this example, relied upon suspended lighting. Like most modern offices, family photographs remain an important part of personalizing what is otherwise a very public space. Notice how they are positioned on the mantle as well as tucked into the oil painting on the wall. Unknown photographer, circa 1910-20.

This photograph, like the preceding example shows how older houses were adapted from gaslights to electricity. The old gas fixture, minus its glass shades, can just barely be seen at the top of the photograph. The electric cord was run along the gas line and then dropped to the floor where additional extension cords would have linked it to lights. This room, featuring a mixture of battered furniture from various periods was clearly designed to be comfortable. The hat on the desk, boots drying to the side of the fireplace and piles of papers everywhere confirm this assumption. The sofa, probably seventy years out of date for the room, seems to have been a convenient filing cabinet. The diplomas, family photographs and calligraphy Bible verse all make the room very homey. An interesting feature is the Victorian strip carpeting–the seam of one section is visible just to the left of the desk, as well as the finely made hearth rug. While the fireplace might have been useable, the absence of any andirons perhaps suggests that it was just for show. Unknown photographer, circa 1900-10.

In contrast to the office in a remodeled home, this next image is a space probably in a commercial office building. While identifying the office has been an elusive task, the stand-up sign on the left is for cosmetics suggesting this firm may have been a wholesale broker of such items. A waiting room for clients was located on the photographer's side of the wooden rail. A roll-top desk–much favored for offices–is located on the right side with worktables in the back. Notice the elaborate hanging clock placed just below the central beam as well as the many suspended light fixtures with bare bulbs. Unknown photographer, circa 1910-20.

While industrial, office and retail positions were common in this period, so were farms, feed stores, cider mills and other agrarian-based businesses. The photographs of farms shown here are typical of central Pennsylvania, but could be located anywhere. Home to a rich and long agricultural tradition, these neat and well-ordered farms are still hallmarks of the success of American farming. Today we think of such areas as the home of the Amish and Old Order Mennonites who farm with horses and without the use of modern appointments including electricity. It is important to remember that everyone farmed like the Amish during most of the nineteenth century.

This photograph, albeit in somewhat damaged condition, shows one of the great hardships of farming in the nineteenth century–drought. The fields in the foreground have only a few sparse stalks of corn. The far field, having been allowed to lay fallow or rest for a season, will be cultivated later in the year or probably the next. In the distance is a typical Pennsylvania German farm building complex. The stone house has a farm bell on the roof to call workers in for a meal. To the right is the large wooden "bank barn" so named for its placement into a soil embankment to facilitate access by wagons to the second level or threshing floor. In the foreground, the farm's owners are positioned just in back of a split rail fence that was in the process of being built. Marked "Ensminger, Druggist and Photographer, Manheim Pa," circa 1870-90.

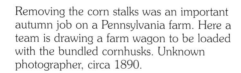

Removing the corn stalks was an important autumn job on a Pennsylvania farm. Here a team is drawing a farm wagon to be loaded with the bundled cornhusks. Unknown photographer, circa 1890.

The Pennsylvania German bank barn was one of the largest types of farm buildings constructed in nineteenth and early twentieth century America. Shown here is an example illustrating the success of this particular form. The animal yard is shown on the ground level with the hay storage located directly above. Built into an embankment of soil on the opposite side, farm wagons could bring hay onto the second floor where it could then be thrown out the doors shown on the side to the animals below. The lean-to on the left was probably for the storage of farm equipment although the slatted area on the far left may be a corncrib. Unknown photographer, circa 1880.

This photo is identified as the cider plant, power house, packing house and office of James Craig in Waynesboro, West Virginia. Even today, the production of apple cider is done fairly close to the orchards. This photograph dated 1913 shows the complex of buildings used to sort apples for production into cider as well as direct shipment to markets. In the foreground, just visible are men using ladders to harvest the apples. Unknown photographer.

Related industries to farming were cider presses used to convert apples into cider and perhaps even onto the next step in the process–Apple Jack. The next image shows a complete apple processing plant from around 1913. Included, of course, are the apple trees in the foreground as well as the sorting buildings for the apples and the cider press. In this period, cider was not pasteurized so it had to be hurried to market to prevent spoilage.

One other important area of work was school. While there are hundreds of ubiquitous photographs of one-room school houses (still functioning in many rural areas well into the twentieth century), the images included here are of the dorm rooms of two different boarding students. The first image is probably far more typical of the life of most boarding students. The furnishings are from Sears Roebuck or a related firm. The absence of family photographs suggests an environment that discouraged personalizing of space although the room is still anything but cold and sterile. The second group of images shows a dorm room at Yale around the turn of the century. The rooms are almost a caricature of what one thinks of when imagining an Ivy League dorm room. Family photographs, Yale memorabilia and a wide range of furnishings are integrated into the space. Both different rooms were created by students using available furniture–either provided by the school or parents–but arranged and embellished to bring a corner of home into their student world.

In many respects, it is the desire to bring a bit of home into the workplace that defines nearly all of these work spaces.

While the exact location of this picture is unknown, the youth of the subjects coupled with the well-worn furniture and school pennant on the wall all are suggestive of a dorm room. The roll top desk, bureau, table and chair are typical of things that could have been purchased rather inexpensively from Sears and Roebuck or any of dozens of other merchants. The painted iron bed appears neither to have a head or footboard that would have been somewhat unusual. The absence of lots of photographs suggests that the school authorities frowned on such things. Unknown photographer, circa 1910.

This series of photographs shows a dorm room at Yale around the turn of the century. All are from an anonymous scrapbook that includes images of later trips to Europe and a dude ranch in Wyoming. These images are a striking contrast to the other dorm room photograph illustrated. Here, family photographs, pennants and memorabilia dominate the room. Grouped together on tables and chairs, this arrangement is frequently called the "Victorian art group" by contemporary scholars. One mystery is the small tags attached to the dozens of art prints hanging on the wall. Perhaps they are titles or calling cards tucked in to the frames. The print of an American Indian chief is suggestive of the turn of the century fascination with American Indians and their plight. The publication of Helen Jackson's *A Century of Dishonor* in 1888 and reprinted many times thereafter was important in drawing the public's attention to the plight of the American Indian. Unknown photographer, circa 1890.

It is difficult to determine if this was a professional or amateur violinist. The determined look on the subject's face and the stoic pose with the violin suggest he was a professional musician. Photographed in a commercial studio, the image is completed with the massive Jacobean Revival armchair and ornate draperies. If he is a professional musician, it is likely that the image would have been used as a promotional advertisement. Marked "Marion, Barristers Hall, Lowell Mass," circa 1880.

This unusual image, taken by L.N. Schmidt of Chicago, shows three men employed in the trades of furniture upholstery and finishing. The man on the right holds brushes for applying the finish. The man on the left holds a small brush or pen, rule and paper for laying out the designs to create faux finishes. The man in the center is either holding a piece of leather to burnish a finish or a sample fabric to upholster a chair. Examples of their ware, including a center table, plant stand (complete with ivy growing up the side) and a faux finish marble plinth, are also shown in what may have been an advertising photograph. Marked "L.N. Schmidt, Chicago," circa 1880.

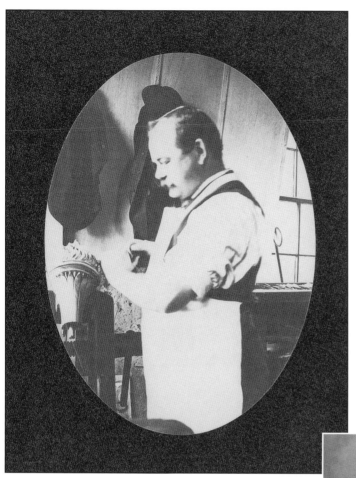

This small photograph shows a professional wood carver creating an example of his decorative work. In the late 1800's, decorative carving, like it had been in the 1790's was a highly prized profession practiced by a limited number of individuals. This specially cut oval photograph was clearly designed to celebrate the skills of this anonymous woodworker. Unknown photographer, circa 1890.

Here is the stuff of the real "old west!" This pair of working cowboys had their photographs taken in the late 1880's or early 1890's in Newkirk, Oklahoma Territory. Without spurs or similar accoutrements, it is difficult to know whether they were truly cowboys or well-dressed day laborers or storekeepers. Marked "Parker, Newkirk, O.T."

The importance of the local sawmill cannot be over-emphasized in the late nineteenth century. Board lumber for flooring, siding and other construction was an important local commodity. This photograph shows a team and driver delivering a load of logs to the mill. The finished board lumber is stacked on the right side of the image. Unknown photographer, circa 1910.

The dark paneled clothing store lit only by hanging oil and gas lamps conveys to us a very different sense than our modern shopping malls. On the left side of the image are suits probably waiting to be picked up by clients since most such places produced custom-made goods. On the right are both empty and filled boxes holding hats, collars and other articles of apparel. Notice the hanging signs on both sides advertising the latest styles and fashions. Unknown location and photographer, circa 1910.

This is clearly the office of a seed or feed company as the seed signs hanging around the walls suggest. The chromed Aladdin lamp on the table–probably with a white milk glass shade–provided the primary illumination outside of the two windows. Natural light was an important aspect of nineteenth and early twentieth century life. Notice how the typing table and stool are positioned as close to the window as possible to take advantage of daylight. The roll-top desk, oak chairs and just visible cast iron stove (on the right) all point to a date around 1900. An interesting curiosity is the horseshoe sitting on the windowsill. It is perhaps a good luck charm (although pointing down so the luck flows out) or maybe a souvenir from a favorite horse. Unknown photographer, circa 1900.

A second feed store is shown in this photograph. The tin pipe running across the room was to vent the smoke out of the stove on the right side. The table with counting house desk resting on it was the preferred desk form for most retail businesses in the nineteenth and early twentieth centuries. Unknown photographer, circa 1910-20.

While stocking a wide range of wares, the interior of this early twentieth century shoe store is far-removed from the displays found in modern stores. The fitting area is on the right with long benches being used for the patrons. Stock is on the shelves to the right with the rear being used by the resident cobbler. This shop probably did repair work and perhaps some custom shoes. Notice the use of the exposed light bulbs hanging from the ceiling. The novelty of electricity was such that exposed bulbs were visible proof of the sophistication of the owner. Unknown photographer, circa 1910.

This richly ornamented jewelry, silver and clock shop is in striking comparison with the shoe store shown previously. The showcases would have been either walnut or probably grained-painted to simulate mahogany. Notice the female sales clerk who would have been available to show women customers various items. This mixing of sexes in a retail space was a new phenomenon during the late nineteenth century. Men had historically selected household furnishings although this changed significantly beginning around the Civil War. Unknown photographer, circa 1900.

In comparison to the richly appointed stores, here is the shop and "manufactory" of a single-owner business. The harness-maker was an important part of nineteenth century life. Like the blacksmith, his place in a community dependent upon horses for transportation, was critical. Hanging above his workbench is a selection of the various kinds of buckles and brasses that he could use. Suspended from the rafters are finished harnesses while pieces in progress line the workbench. Unknown photographer, circa 1910.

Another important rural business was raising domesticated fish. Not exclusively a late twentieth century phenomenon, commercial inland fishing existed for many years. This example, near the Pennsylvania town of New Providence, shows the various pens and gates used to move and keep the fish. The species is unknown although shad may be one possibility. Unknown photographer, circa 1910.

Chapter 3
The Stereocard

Perhaps no other force influenced interior decoration in the late nineteenth and early twentieth centuries as much as the stereocard. These popular parlor amusements introduced historic houses, exotic lands, fantasy and literary scenes and more to widely diverse audiences. The process was quite simple. Two identical images were mounted side-by-side on a narrow card. They were viewed through a pair of special binoculars to produce a three dimensional image of the subject. Most stereoviewers were small and handheld. There were, however, large double and even quadruple stereoviewers produced so that an entire family might view scenes at the same time. In addition, the ease in mass-producing stereocards made them a popular retail item even among local photographers.

OVER.   MAIN BUILDING PHILA CEN'T

This stereocard is titled "The Main Building of the Philadelphia Centennial Exposition of 1876." Although events such as the Philadelphia Sanitary Fair preceded the Centennial, the grandeur of the Exposition marked it as the real beginning of the popularization of national expositions or fairs in the United States. The general availability of photographs–and stereocards in particular–meant that audiences across the nation could view scenes of the Exposition. Marked "U.S. Stereoscopic View Advertising Company," circa 1876.

An interesting category of cards were those designed to teach a moral, or perhaps an immoral, lesson to the viewer. Several of the cards shown in the images that follow were produced to either teach a lesson or titillate the viewer. Some, like the drunken or philandering husband, were clearly designed as visual morality plays. Others like the woman undressing after the dance or the couple kissing on their wedding night had a slightly erotic edge meant for an adult male audience.

Another group of cards in this series are of great, and perhaps not-so-great interiors, from the 1880's to around 1910. Stereocards of the White House not only introduced the American public to the "President's home" but also were important in establishing decorating styles and trends elsewhere. Similarly, the parlor of the artist

Samuel Bell Waugh, while produced for a much smaller audience, introduced the viewer to the home of an American artist–and quite obviously a collector as well. Finally, there were even cards produced for individual families that showed details of their own parlors. While such cards may not have influenced others, they in and of themselves, are interesting texts that reveal the priority that interior decoration took during this period.

Through the 1930's, sets were still being produced and enjoyed during the evening. With the outbreak of World War II and the subsequent appearance of the television, cards rapidly disappeared. The irony of the stereocard was that it reappeared during the 1970's as the Viewmaster. Final proof that what goes around, comes around.

No. 25   Pennsylvania State Building
Copyrighted, 1904, by T. W. Ingersoll.

Stereocards of public buildings, like the Philadelphia Centennial Hall and the Pennsylvania State Capitol in Harrisburg, were among the first widespread photographic views of the United States. This scene, dated 1904, is typical of early twentieth century stereocards in that it shows people actively engaged in passing through the landscape background. Earlier cards were usually devoid of people. Marked "T.W. Ingersoll."

Although untitled, this European scene of peasant life is typical of the images that brought exotic parts of the world into the parlors of Victorian America. Carefully staged by the photographer to include as many exotic elements as possible (the wooden shoes as an example), such cards were the mainstay of the worldview stereocard sets that were sold. Marked " James Cremer Photographer and Publisher, Philadelphia," circa 1880.

Stereocards also could be produced for a very local audience. This scene is of a picnic in Harrisburg Pennsylvania sometime in the 1870s and 1880s. Unsigned and undated, it probably was produced by a local photographer and made available for sale to the picnic attendees for a nominal fee. Unknown photographer.

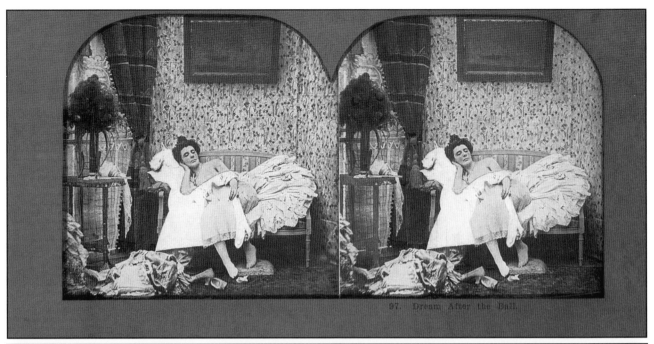

97. Dream After the Ball.

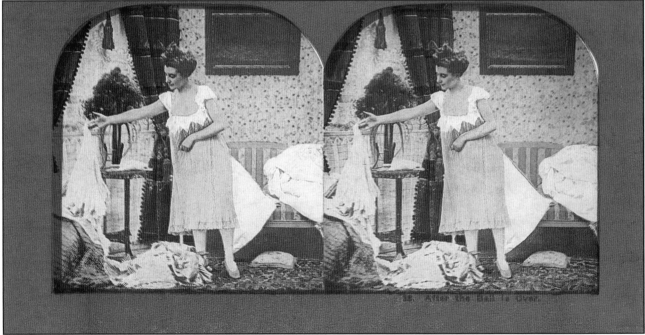

98. After the Ball Is Over.

This pair of cards is from a large sequence that were probably produced for a male audience. The young woman, in various stages of undress, is shown relaxing after a large ball. Notice the strong use of color as the background. While it is difficult to know if these were accurate color choices to the original scene, it is amazingly bright color scheme and perhaps fairly accurate to many interiors in the late Victorian period. Unknown photographer, circa 1900.

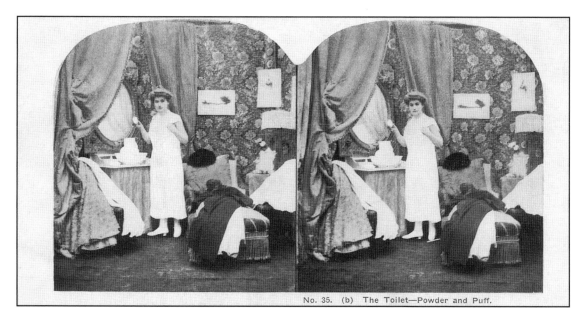

No. 35. (b) The Toilet—Powder and Puff.

This scene is also slightly erotically titillating with the subject in state of semi-undress. The card is titled *The Toilet–Powder and Puff, No. 35*. The color choice, pink and green, was a favorite of lady's dressing rooms in the early twentieth century. Unknown photographer, circa 1900.

No. 30. (a) "Good-Bye, Dearest; I'll Be Home Early."

No. 31. (b) Mr. Small Returns Quite Early.

This pair of cards was produced as part of a larger sequence of cards sold as a set. The subject, depending upon your perspective, can be viewed as either humorous or moralistic. The first card is titled *Good-Bye Dearest, I'll be Home Early* while the second, clearly to show subsequent events, is titled *Mr. Small Returns Quite Early*. The Gothic hall chair may have been suggestive of religious overtones in the card as was the art print on the wall. Unknown photographers, circa 1900.

These two cards have the same basic theme and composition although published by different firms. Both address issues of marital infidelity in a comic manner. The subject is a husband and maid involved in a tryst while the wife comes bursting into the room. The appearance of alcoholic beverages –appearing to be wine or beer–on the table further adds to the suggestion of vice. Interestingly, in both cards, the maid wears striped stockings perhaps indicating her "loose" nature. The colored card is captioned "No. 44, Mrs. Brown Returns Unexpected/Copyrighted 1898 by T.W. Ingersoll." The black and white card is titled "Mrs. Jones Comes Back Unexpectedly/Copyright Griffith and Griffith."

Alone at Last in four languages is printed on the reverse of this card showing a couple relaxing after their wedding. This card would have been somewhat scandalous in its day since kisses were only just beginning to be shown in popular imagery. Marked "Strokemeyer and Wyman, New York, copyright 1897."

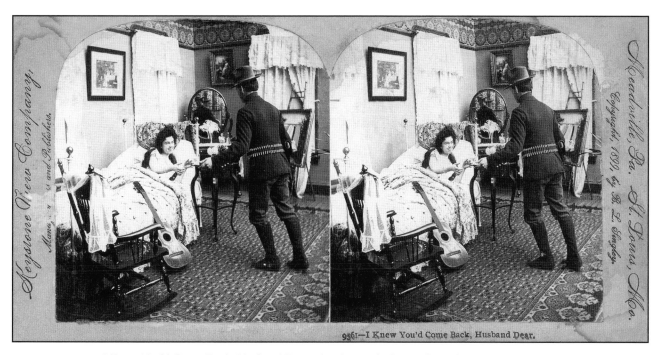

I Knew You'd Come Back, Husband Dear titles this card where a Spanish American War veteran is shown entering his bedroom and surprising his wife. Amazingly, the soldier apparently rushed home right from getting off the boat from Cuba or the Philippines since he still is carrying a cartridge belt and revolver. The scene is quasi-erotic although it is tempered by the fact that the title notes that it is her husband. Marked "B.L. Singley, copyright 1899."

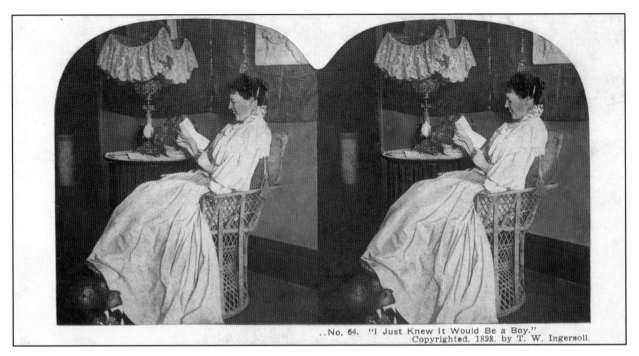

..No. 64. "I Just Knew It Would Be a Boy."
Copyrighted, 1898. by T. W. Ingersoll.

I just knew it would be a boy is a stereocard from the same series as the image of *I'll be home early*. Notice that the same props have been re-arranged in the room. The table and puffy shaded lamp are now arranged as a little niche for the reading of a letter. The bear head–clearly part of a bearskin rug–adds a rather bizarre touch to this card. Marked "T.W. Ingersoll, copyrighted 1898."

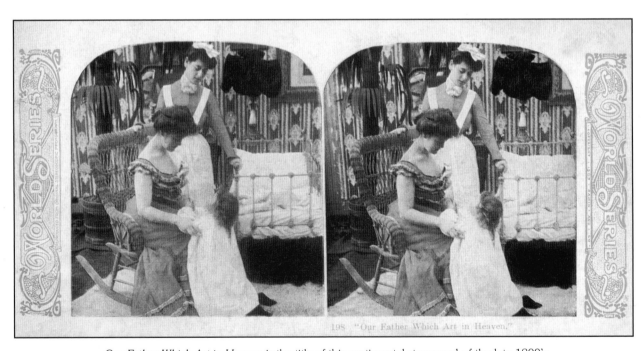

198 "Our Father Which Art in Heaven."

Our Father Which Art in Heaven is the title of this sentimental stereocard of the late 1800's. Of particular interest is the use of the wicker rocker, painted iron bed and fabric covered light fixture in the background. While it would be logical to surmise that these were typical furnishings of the late nineteenth century, it is more than likely that they were convenient to the photograph's studio. The riotous wallpaper is revealing about the bright color choices that were probably common in this period. Marked "Rawin and Company, copyrighted 1904."

Library, President's Mansion and *State Dining Room in President's Mansion* are the titles of this pair of cards dating from 1900 and showing the interior of the White House. The dining room is grand and elegant in appearance while the library appears to contain a mixture of styles and a near total absence of personal possessions. Like the Centennial and Pennsylvania Capitol stereocards, images such as this provided the public with an insider's view of the important landmarks of the day. They also were a source of decorating inspiration for many homeowners. Both marked "J. F. Jarvis of Washington DC," circa 1900.

This privately produced card is of the interior of the art studio of American painter Samuel Bell Waugh (1814-1885) in New Jersey. While the popularity and distribution of this card is unknown, the fact that it does exist suggests that the homes of artists were also of interest to many Americans. The room itself is a tribute to the Victorian art group concept as every item from statues to books on the floor are artfully arranged to convey a sense of disorderly order to the room. Unknown photographer, circa 1880.

Opposing page:
These three cards, all printed by different firms, show a wide range of Victorian parlor statuary. Such images, beyond providing basic interest to those seeking to view a range of different types of art, also introduced homeowners to the range of statues that they might think of purchasing. While perhaps not being able to afford–or find a place for a 6' classical woman–they could obtain plaster or Parian copies at more reasonable prices. Unknown photographers, circa 1876-90.

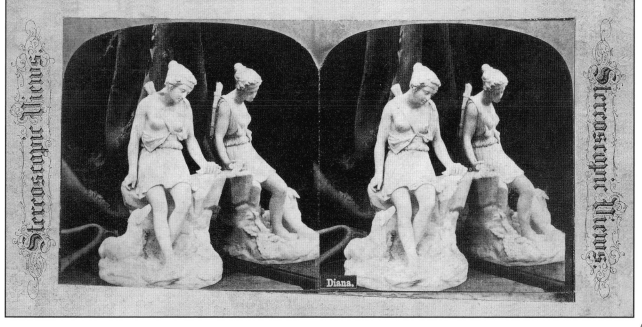

Titled *The Residence of R. S. Sturgis at Newport, Rhode Island*, this view shows two rooms and dates from the 1880's. The rooms are decorated in an exotic taste with such features as a Turkish table and Chinese floor vase in the foreground and a wide range of plants including Calendula in the back. Notice how the matched paintings are hung on the draperies that divide the two rooms. Unknown photographer, circa 1880.

Titled in pencil on the reverse as *The Residence of S. B. Fales*, this is a wonderful view of an affluent family's double parlor. The paintings are fitted out salon style with smaller works near the floor and large canvases on top. The library table in the foreground is attributable to the Philadelphia cabinetmaker George Henkels who produced high style Renaissance Revival furnishings. The obelisk on the table, like many of the other furnishings, was probably brought home from a Grand Tour to Europe. The most striking feature of the card is the use of the American flag bunting as the separation between the rooms as well as small flags hanging inside the doorframes. Perhaps the photograph was taken to celebrate the Centennial in 1876 or similar occasions. Unknown photographer, circa 1880.

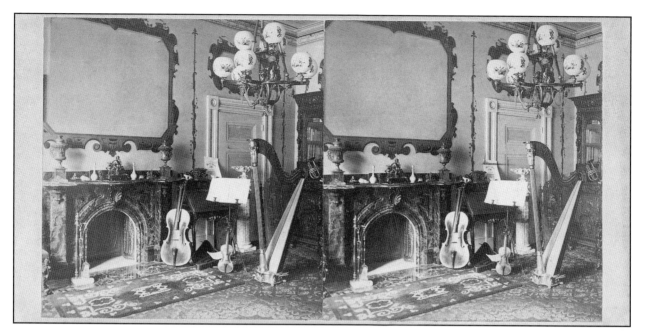

This card was acquired with the preceding example and may be the music room in this same great house. Certainly the quality of furnishings, while not as abundant as in the parlor, are of the same level as the other image. The French desk and Italian mirror may have been imported from Europe or perhaps made in an eastern American city. Notice the hearth rug laid down in front of the now-empty fireplace. Unknown photographer, circa 1880.

This bedroom, decorated in a Renaissance or Jacobean Revival taste, features an unusual ceiling canopy. It may have been a grand touch to this impressive room. The chairs in the room were probably part of a parlor set although they have found a place scattered among the matching bedroom suite. Unknown photographer, circa 1880.

Chapter 4
The Parlor

Images of Victorian parlors provide the best glimpse into everyday life in the late nineteenth century. The separate room reserved for "state occasions" was a necessary feature of every home. With changing architectural styles, in particular the rise of the bungalow, these rooms became less and less formal. By the 1910's, the parlor was being used for regular family activities rather than kept closed for all except company.

Parlors were not strictly places to go and sit. Rather they were a visual vocabulary of the wealth and morals of the family that lived there. They were three-dimensional representations of the story of the family from birth to death. In the corner might be a black draped photograph of a newly deceased family member. Next to it would be a portrait of the youngest–and still living–child in the family. A Bible might point to the spirituality of the family while a host of flowers and plants showed the care and attention of the family to their parlor.

This double parlor home, probably in Minneapolis Minnesota, is interesting insofar as the walls, floors and other architectural features are quite elaborate while the furnishings remain simple –almost to the point of being out of scale with the remainder of the room. It is as if the family lavished its attention on the wooden ball curtain, strip carpeting and ornate wallpaper borders but then could only afford simple commercially available chairs and furnishings. The statue is by the popular sculptor John Rogers' and was titled *Madam, Your Mother Craves a Word with You*. Patented in 1883, the scene is from Shakespeare's Romeo and Juliet. Such pieces were intended to demonstrate to visitors how well-read and versed in the classics this particular family was. Signed on bottom "Photographed by M.S. Amy, Minneapolis, MN"

The arrangement of parlors, while appearing to be random, was carefully proscribed. Balance and symmetry appear to be important based upon the surviving images although it is difficult to be certain that some room settings were not specifically created just for the photographer. While to our eye, clutter abounds in these rooms. It is important to remember that random clutter was not part of daily life at this time. Objects were arranged in "art groups" around central themes. An easel might have a photograph draped in a paisley shawl with ivy tendrils woven into the back. This was done quite deliberately to create a grouping of objects whereby no individual object stood out but rather that there was a unified design in effect. Even today, with our emphasis on sparse modern interiors, the art group continues to be an important part of decoration. One need only look at the careful arrangement of books and candles on a coffee table to realize the long-lived effect of this concept.

It is also interesting to note the mixing of periods and furniture suites in the majority of these rooms. Many textbooks would like us to believe that family's purchased matching parlor suites of furniture when they were married and that things never changed. In scanning these images, the near total lack of matching sets is quite apparent. Instead, it appears that families had few qualms about mixing and matching styles, periods and forms. In fact, the story of a family's prosperity can be read by the range of furnishings in a room. A Victorian parlor table of the 1860's might have been a family piece or hand-me-down while the little oak side table is perhaps a brand-new acquisition from a local merchant or even through a catalog.

It is also important to recognize that these photographs show a selection of how many Americans lived in the 1880 to 1920 period. The furnishings to many modern antique collectors appear to be common and ordinary. Where are the parlors showing furniture by the leading cabinetmakers such as John Henry Belter? He was an expensive maker in his day and the furnishings that he produced were not available on a widespread basis. What is interesting is that many of the rooms do include copies of furnishings made by large name cabinetmakers. Like today, we can purchase an expensive piece from the successors of the Stickley firm or we can purchase an inexpensive example from Futon. The issue is that both carry the same aesthetic–the difference being cost and construction.

A look at these photographs is a walk back in time to a world very different than our own. Cleanliness in rooms was not nearly as important as it is today, Few window screens, inadequate cleaning products and an intensive lifestyle centered around basic necessities meant that the whiter-than-white mentality of today was not true then. One of the most frequently asked questions by visitors to historic house museums is "how did they clean all this stuff?" The answer is that they didn't do it! Certainly when it came time for cleaning, the rich had their servants to tend to this duty. If the family did clean their home, it was not on the intensive schedule that our post-modern world of today insists we follow. Hand-pumped vacuum cleaners, limited cleaning products and coal furnaces surely meant that dust and dirt were a daily, and acceptable, part of life. In fact, one almost wonders if the rich and crusty patina that collectors today seek in antiques is really a manifestation of housekeeping, or the lack thereof, practices in the nineteenth century.

Technological changes also played an important role in these rooms. Early parlors focused on the large central table with an equally large oil lamp. The mass introduction of gas fixtures by the second half of the century meant that every corner of the parlor could be well lit. Electricity then came along and changed everything. When houses were first wired for electricity, the cable was snaked along the existing gas lines. The results can be seen in many of these photographs as there is a characteristic hanging extension cord that descends from the ceiling chandelier down to the floor and branches out to floor lamps. Although there were no recorded deaths from exploding gas light fixtures in a home, the negative campaigning of the early electric companies convinced the public of the safety of the new form of illumination. So popular was the electric light bulb that decorative shades or covers do not appear for some years after its introduction into homes. Rather bare bulbs–perceived as ugly to us today–were seen as visual symbols of this new technology.

At first glance, this appears to be a parlor of the 1890's. A closer look reveals a wicker chair of around 1910 and several "Gibson Girl" type art prints hanging in the room. The image might be titled "amusements in the parlor" as the stack of books (piled high on the center table) and the parlor organ reveal two of the chief occupations for families during this period. The most interesting feature is the conversion of one of the arms of the gas chandelier into an electric fixture. Such changes were popular as families often left the gas fixtures in-place so that they could be used again if electricity proved to be too difficult. Unknown photographer, titled on reverse "Picture of James Willson Doran, grandmother and mother, 1115 Reaney Street, St. Paul, Minn., 1914."

Heat was another issue that was changing in homes. While early heating systems had been developed in some homes by the end of the Civil War, the popularization of central heating does not occur for some time. Families in many rural locations continued to use large, ornamental parlor stoves for heat well into the early twentieth century. Perhaps this was due to a distrust of the new systems and their start-up costs or more than likely it was a result of a traditional aesthetic that saw the parlor stove, like the center table and the pump organ, as critical design elements.

The parlors shown here exhibit a mixture of furnishings and styles. Some have very definite design precedents in Moorish or Middle Eastern tastes while others reach back to America's own colonial past. I have tried to separate those rooms which truly would have been described as "Colonial" or "Arts and Crafts" from those which mix and match many design elements. These definitions are purely my own and probably would not have been how the original owners described their spaces.

This lithographed trade card for a portrait studio provides us with a double glimpse into late Victorian parlor decoration. The layering of fabrics, objects and textures was common in parlors of the late nineteenth century and this stylized example is no exception. It is doubtful that any child, let alone one with a paint brush and palette, would be allowed into a parlor, but the effect was to create a scene of domestic tranquility for the buyer. The reverse advertised E.P. Waite and Company's services to paint portraits of sitters. The popularity of photography, while seriously hurting portrait commissions in the 1850's and 1860's nevertheless rebounded by the end of the century. A status symbol, by that point, portraits again became an important part of the décor of those who were affluent, or at least aspiring to be. Unknown printer, circa 1890.

Although there is some speculation about who popularized the use of the Christmas tree in America, it is likely that Prince Albert–consort to Queen Victoria of England–introduced it to a mass audience. This scene, dating from the early twentieth century, shows a typical table-top tree decorated with cards, a few balls, popcorn and possibly paper flowers. Floor-length trees were not common during this period. Notice the background arrangement of what appears to be a rubber plant and possibly a fern. This was part of the Victorian concept of the "art group" whereby objects had to be grouped together in order to create harmony within a room. Marked "A.E.Riley, Coshockton, O."

Here is perhaps the ultimate Victorian sitting room. The use of fabric is overwhelming including on the floor (oriental rugs and an animal pelt), the cushions on the daybed (appearing mostly to be ruffled silks) and even the hand-embroidered curtains. The banjo was a common feature of Victorian domestic life and probably was played by the woman whose bedchamber is beyond. The furniture is a mixture of styles including a Renaissance Revival bed and washstand and an oak Colonial Revival rocker and a wicker armchair. Signed on the reverse in pencil "Home of Walter and Alice, Portland, 125 Spring Street." Unknown photographer.

The parlor of this home (located at 90 High street in Portland, Maine) is a mixture of a number of late nineteenth century styles and movements. The windsor side chair, brass andirons, and Adamesque plaster frieze were all inspired by the Colonial Revival. However, the art groups and swagged fireplace along with the chairs on the right side of the photograph, are all indicative of late Victorian art groups and specifically the Renaissance Revival style. The firewood ready to be burned and the stacks of correspondence and books on the table suggest that this was a popular room for the family. Stamped on reverse " A.D. Currier, 385 Congress street, Portland, Maine."

Another identified parlor is the Orland and Lillian Goodwin residence at "635 G Street, North East, Washington D.C. Taken on May 29, 1897," the room is outfitted in simple middle class furnishings. The strip carpeting on the floor identifiable by the seams running on either side of Mr. Goodwin's feet, is typical of the period. An animal rug is located in the bay window. The table is a mystery as it appears to be either a high quality European early nineteenth century table or perhaps an equally expensive copy. The rockers, piano stool and other appointments were mass-produced an available in many stores. Notice that the shades on the gas jets have been removed suggesting that the home had been outfitted with electricity by this point. Stamped on reverse "H.A. Farnham, View Photographer, 936 F Street, N.W., Washington D.C."

This parlor shows a room set for afternoon tea. The tête-à-tête is drawn up with lots of cushions by a small table set with cups and a hot water kettle on stand. The fireplace surround features a range of late Victorian ceramics and a monumental clock and candelabra set. The walls are hung, gallery style, with inexpensive art prints. The center point of the room is the stuffed flag pillow that helps in dating the room to the last decade of the nineteenth century. Unknown photographer.

This parlor, dating from around 1900, is an interesting study in conspicuous consumption. The family is probably middle class based upon the furnishings and have staged an image that shows a tremendous number of their household items. The older child sits at the piano while a younger one rests on her father's lap with a toy piano nearby under the chair. Pillows for the children to rest on or the adults to use for their feet are "scattered" (probably intentionally placed) on the floor. Photographs of the children flank the walls with a central parlor table covered in probably a beautifully figured cloth. Notice the animal pelt on the floor being used underneath the lady's feet. Use of animal pelts as throw rugs was a common occurrence in turn of the century parlors throughout the United States. Unknown photographer.

Compare this parlor with the one shown previously. Dating from the same time (in fact this example is dated October 7th, 1899), this room shows a marked difference in design. Whereas the previous image reflected late Victorian design features, this room–while furnished with similar items– relates to the new sparseness of the Colonial Revival and Mission styles. The strip carpeting and throw rug along with the Eastlake chairs and parlor table closely mirror the other image. Notice, however, that the table is not placed in the center of the window, room or photograph. Rather it is set to the side. Further, the plants are sparsely placed in a symmetrical arrangement around the windows. Unknown photographer.

This image shows a parlor and adjoining dining room from around 1900. Notice the use of the American flag, photographs and greeting cards on the mantle as decoration. The oak chairs in the dining room would have been retailed as "colonial" in taste. A cloth fire screen has been pulled in front of the opening, although probably not to prevent sparks from flying out but rather to hide the opening during the day. Unknown photographer.

This darkly photographed parlor is an intriguing image. The wallpaper and border were in the aesthetic taste of the late 1800's. Notice the papered ceiling as well. The massive and ornate parlor stove in the corner provides a focal point for the room although the small center table–a holdover in design from the 1860's–is meant to be the center-point of the room. In the adjacent parlor or music room is an upright piano and a statue of Venus. The oak chairs and wicker suggest a date of around 1900. Unknown photographer.

This stereocard is quite amusing in that the photographer probably told everyone in the image to focus on some distant object and not to look at the camera. The result is a scene that is suggestive of a momentary pause caused by a loud irritating fly in the room. The furnishings are a mixture of styles including a Rococo revival sofa and table of the 1860's and a wicker side chair of the 1880's or 1890.s' Unknown photographer.

Looking at this cabinet card photograph, it is difficult to determine whether it is an American or European scene. The German steins on the shelves as well as the Black Forest clock on the wall suggest at the least a Continental European scene although the image was found with other American images on the West Coast. The lesson is that by the end of the nineteenth century, styles were becoming so uniformly accepted around the world that it is difficult to determine ethnic origins. Unknown photographer, circa 1900.

The image of "Little Willie," who was a schoolmate of the author's grandfather, is particularly interesting. The parlor dates from around 1905 and the furnishings would have been described as colonial. The brass claw on glass ball foot of the table was meant to copy the eighteenth century carved mahogany ball and claw feet of the Chippendale period. The rocker, with its multitude of carvings and turnings, again was a mixture of a number of earlier styles. Behind is a framed photograph or art print that was artfully draped in cloth–not for mourning–but simply to create its own art unit. Unknown photographer.

Taken from a studio photographer's notebook, this image is a joy for the photo researcher. Titled "Philadelphia; 187 W. Huntingdon Street, Miss Mimi Gunis, Mrs. Hozey" and dated October 17, 1893, it provides an intimate glimpse into a middle class parlor. The symmetry of the room is perhaps the most striking feature and one that dominated parlor of this period. The parlor organ is on the left with the fireplace on the right. Matching portraitures and tables neatly balance the room. It is likely that these are two sisters–one of which may be a widow–and who are now living together. Unknown photographer.

Probably taken in the coal country of northern Pennsylvania, this family is gathered in their finery around the fireplace of their home. On the right is a draped image of a child who probably died young but whose image was incorporated into the family group photo. It is difficult to tell if there is actually a fireplace and mantel behind or whether it is simply a draped shelf. The greatest mystery is the box on the left side of the photograph. Appearing like a modern television, it may have been a religious altar. Unknown photographer, circa 1910.

This intriguing image shows a parlor–probably from the west coast–that is decorated with a wonderful abundance of plants and fabric. A corner has been created using a fabric curtain or screen from which cattails and reeds are used as decoration. An animal rug is by the fireplace and Japanese mums decorate the mantel. The side table would have probably been sold as "colonial" in style although it mixes several artistic periods. Unknown photographer, circa 1910-20.

This photograph is a wonderful study in the uses of light in late nineteenth century homes. This carefully staged photograph has a young lady reading a book–probably her Bible–by the light of a fabric draped oil lamp. Such lamps provided weak illumination and it is unlikely that she could have read much by this fixture. Behind her are fixed, louvered wooden shutters that were used to regulate the passage of air and light into a house. The use of shutters, both inside and out, was critical in maintaining the necessary temperature for a home during summer and winter. The fabric roller blind, which is drawn to aid the photographer, was critical in lighting rooms. The spool table was popular from the 1850's onward although the wicker chair that she is seated at is from 1900. Unknown photographer.

The electric light and the attire of the gentleman in this photograph point to a date in 1930's although the furnishings of this room would not have been out of place in the 1880's. The layered or gallery-style of painting display was a common feature of Victorian parlors. The Jacobean linen press was a fitting antique for what appear to be Old Master paintings. Unlike the 1880's, the decorative objects used in this space are not vases or glass but rather a soup tureen, beer mug and candlesticks with and without candles. The fabric-draped light was either made of or copied from a seventeenth century ecclesiastical candlestick. Unknown photographer.

These two photographs, dated 1926 incorporate the same electric reading light and were carefully staged probably by an amateur photographer. The older couple–probably the parents of the younger woman–were symmetrically balanced around their fireplace. The home is probably older than the image, and may be even older than the couple, as the carved mantle suggests a date from the 1860's or 1870's. The room's sparse decorations would perhaps have been called "colonial." The young girl sits in front of a window where the top shutters are drawn but the bottom ones are open revealing that the photo was taken at night. The chair and desk are in the Arts and Crafts style and were probably purchased new for her. Notice the electric cord coming out of the gas jet nozzle and going down to the floor to power the lamp. A hanging electric light fixture can also be seen overhead. Unknown photographer.

The living room of our modern world, as seen in this photograph, probably dates from the 1930's or 1940's. The center table has been replaced with the coffee table–both furniture forms being distinctive and functional to their times. The parlor organ has been replaced by the grand piano. Art prints decorate the walls to provide both a moral lesson and to serve as a status symbol. The biggest difference is the walls and floors. Colonial white or a related light color has replaced the dark wall coverings of the Victorian era. The strip carpeting has been replaced with a large oriental rug that in turn will ultimately be replaced by wall-to-wall carpeting. Still, the functions of the room–as a place for entertaining and display–remains the same as it was in the late nineteenth century. Unknown photographer.

Fewer photographs of dining rooms survive than those of parlors. The gentleman in this photograph is relaxing in his favorite rocking chair placed in a corner of the dining room. Perhaps he is a bachelor or widower as the room has a distinctive look that is suggestive of strictly male occupancy. The bow-front china cabinet holds what today would be thought of as the "good china." Of interest are the wealth of details in the photograph including the ceramic or metal dogs on the floor, the pipes and humidor and the elaborate footstool. Unknown photographer.

Probably this scene is of a dining room in a boarding house or hotel and dates from the 1880's. The table is set for the next meal complete with he castor set holding various condiments. The room is a study in symmetry and balance with pairs of plants, chairs and art prints decorating the space. Stamped on the back "The Commercial Photographing Co., No. 725 Washington Street, Boston, Mass."

Chapter 5

Looking Backward

The changes begun in the late nineteenth century have long been seen as the precursor of our own modern era. Industrial change brought about a new level of prosperity that not only extended to the Mellons and Rockefellers but also to a newly affluent middle class.

At the same time as there was such industrial growth, there was also a contemporary appearance of such modern phenomena as labor and social unrest, imperialism and expansionism, and in terms of the arts–a mass production of various historic styles. Many saw the impact of these issues as undermining the very core of American society. The result was a popular look backward in time to a perceived period when people were in touch with their agrarian roots and the "unsavory" aspects of modernity did not exist. From this anti-modern movement came what is perhaps the most long-lived of all the late nineteenth century styles–the Colonial Revival. While other styles have come and gone, the "early American" or "country" look remains as popular today as it was one hundred fifty years ago.

Scholars have looked at the 1876 American Centennial exposition in Philadelphia as the introduction into widespread popular culture of the Colonial Revival aesthetic. While a small number (in comparison to the overall American population) of people came to the Centennial, the impact of inexpensive commercial lithography and mass-produced photographic images brought the exposition to a huge audience. Photos, prints, scarves and books were mass-produced and marketed throughout the United States. As a result, Americans became enthused–in a way never previously seen–with their own heritage.

Popular mass-produced photographic images can really be argued to be the other major factor contributing to the impact of the Colonial Revival. From the stereocards marketed of Centennial Hall in 1876 to the staged interiors created by Wallace Nutting as well as many others during the early twentieth century, photography promoted the early American look to a staggering audience. In my family, like many others, hand-colored photographs of pastoral scenes or colonial interiors were standard gifts for wedding presents throughout the first decades of the twentieth century. These images, beyond introducing America's heritage to the audience, also established certain conventions of decoration and design. One example is the long-debated myth of the rifle hanging on the hearth over the fireplace opening. Early staged photographs of interiors invariably portray the rifle hanging over the hearth. Questions about accidentally discharging the rifle from the heat of the fireplace and access during an attack notwithstanding, the photographs of this period engrained this image in the popular psyche and over the mantle of many contemporary homes.

Titled *A Newport Home in 1790*, this commercially produced photograph was of a type that was a key source of inspiration for homemakers. Wallace Nutting and many others marketed such images to audiences throughout the United States although most depicted New England homes. The imagery conveyed by these views of the past continues to influence American concepts of the colonial period. The women huddled around the fireplace working at a spinning wheel with a large log set to boil the kettle and the gun over the fireplace. We now know that many of these settings were the complete and total artificial creations of commercial photographers who used them in selling photographs. In fact, a close examination of the objects seemingly casually set around the room reveals a definite order that was far more in keeping with the Victorian art group concept that anything existing in the eighteenth century. Stamped on the reverse "Holloway Instantaneous Portfolio Photographers," circa 1910.

Today, we recognize the Colonial Revival as a style that is distinctive and unique. The homes and rooms that reflect this style are a mixture of eighteenth century furniture married with the Victorian design concept of the art group. The result is a style that used either antique or reproduction furniture mixed with a staggering quantity of decorative accessories to create a homogeneous colonial room. The irony of the Colonial Revival is that it was a style that used more furnishings in one home than most eighteenth century towns collectively owned. It was a style that seemed almost in contradiction to itself as it both celebrated eighteenth century simplicity as well as late nineteenth century conspicuous consumption of goods. However, that mix seemed (and still does) to strike a cord with the audience leading to the overwhelming popularity of the movement.

The prevalence of the Colonial Revival suggests a deeper impact for the style. Interestingly, every point in the late nineteenth and twentieth centuries where there has been societal unrest there has been a corresponding rebirth of some variant of this style. During the late 1890's, golden oak furniture loosely patterned on eighteenth century designs became popular for use in stone and frame colonial houses and bungalows. During the 1920's, the Colonial Revival hit a particular highpoint as Midwestern companies produced quantities of black painted Jacobean influenced furniture. The black paint simulated the oxidized finish of the original green pigments used on period furniture. Today, it can be seen in the abundance of lawn sheep, colonial candles in every window, the use of the flag as a folk art motif, and the revival of interest in early American handcrafts. Again, perhaps as modernity strikes us in a discordant way, we tend to look back towards an earlier period as somehow better or more honest.

Whatever the reason for the Colonial Revival's timeless popularity, it was and still is the dominant decorating style in this country. As you look upon the images in this chapter, I suspect that in many cases you will see familiar sights from your own experience. It is a style that is here to stay.

Analyzing a room is always difficult since we don't know how the original owners would have described their furnishings or even if they were aware of the stylistic names that we so easily use today. The furnishings in this dining room would have been described in catalogs as colonial. Certainly the table is derived from the Sheraton style of the early nineteenth century. However the bold curves of the sideboard and the chairs relate far more to the naturalism of the Art Nouveau style of the late nineteenth century. All made in oak, the set could have been purchased piecemeal or as a suite from either a local store or through a catalog. Unknown photographer, circa 1900.

These three images show what would have been quite an amazing room. The discovery of King Tutankhamun's tomb in 1922 created a flurry of interest in all things Egyptian. While there had been an Egyptian Revival in the nineteenth century, it did not come close to the popularity and fervor of the 1930's revival. The rooms show the space of someone, probably the young woman, who clearly celebrates the modern world. The radio and phonograph are clearly modern appointments as are the beaded fringes on the lamps. Perhaps the most revealing aspect of the photo is that the young woman has her feet up on the daybed–a pose that would not have been permitted in an image thirty years earlier. However, the arrangement of the furnishings is still derived from the late nineteenth century period. The symmetrical clustering of objects and prints in art groups is perhaps the best evidence of this holdover in style. Unknown photographer, circa 1930.

This photograph shows the table, chair and communion service belonging to the Donegal Presbyterian Church located near Lancaster, Pennsylvania. Images like this were probably produced for members of the congregation as a celebration of the antiquity of the church. They also served the dual purpose of being inspirations for antique collectors and furniture designers who sought to own such pieces as a way of acquiring not only a link to the past but perhaps a touch of local gentility. Unknown photographer, circa 1900.

This stereocard is of the hallway at Mt. Vernon around 1880 or 1890. Recent research has shown that the original paint scheme of this hall was dramatically different than the dark woodwork and patterned wallpaper would suggest. Commercially produced cards, like this example, were important sources of inspiration for home owners and decorators. Stamped on reverse "Luke C. Dillon, Authorized Photographer."

"Living Room" The Randell Tabern, Painesville, Ohio. A Tavern since 1810.

DINING ROOM, JOHN ALDEN HOUSE, BUILT 1653, DUXBURY, MASS.

PARLOR-RUFUS PUTNAM HOUSE

As Americans became interested in their past as well as having the means–thanks to the automobile–to explore it, post cards like these became important sources of design. All three rooms, by eighteenth century standards, are horribly over-furnished with a mixture of items that may or may not be period. The arrangement of the various pieces has far more in common with the "art group" concept. All are by unknown photographers, circa 1920-30.

Titled *Living Room* and *The Playground*, these companion photographs show a circa 1900 Colonial Revival home probably in Pennsylvania. The furnishings are a mixture of several styles and periods although they predominantly reflect late eighteenth and early nineteenth century decorative arts. The kettle used to hold firewood is still considered a fundamental hallmark of a Colonial Revival space. Note the symmetry of the spaces, the white woodwork and the use of oriental rugs on the floors. These are all Colonial Revival features that differed strongly from the dark woodwork, wall-to-wall strip carpeting and the asymmetry of Victorian interiors. Unknown photographer, circa 1900.

Opposing page:
It is difficult to know if this scene is from either a historic house museum or a private residence. The fire-bucket hanging under the stair, the ancestral portrait on the far wall and the school bell on the radiator all point to a twentieth century attempt to re-create an eighteenth century space. The hat rack on the left and the barely visible table and art group in the distant room are clearly Victorian room appointments. The white woodwork and dark floors and staircase are hallmarks of Colonial Revival interiors. Signed "Smith," dated 1924.

This pair of photographs shows the living room and dining room of a home that reflects the eclectic tastes of the Colonial Revival style. The living room features such early American icons as the Nathaniel Currier print of George Washington, the white woodwork, the reproduction desk and creative adaptation in the settee. Notice the use of a lithophane or translucent sheet hung in front of the electrical wall light. The dining room has a set of reproduction chairs and a Victorian floor mirror. The Colonial Revival, as a historically based revival style, was not afraid to incorporate elements of Victorian design as well. Perhaps judged to be family heirlooms, such pieces were important parts of Colonial Revival design. Circa 1910, unknown photographer, 9" x 7"

This is the first of series of five photographs taken inside a home–probably a bungalow on the west coast–around 1920 or 1930. The architecture of the room–particularly the exposed brick of the fireplace and the tile of the hearth–are far more in keeping with the Arts and Crafts movement than that of the Colonial Revival. The open floor plan of the rooms, along with the use of large windows, are also indicative of this style. On the West Coast, where there was an obvious absence of eighteenth century New England farmhouses, bungalows often were interpreted in a colonial mode. At least one manifestation of the Arts and Crafts movement looked back to seventeenth century design for its inspiration so to have colonial furnishings in a bungalow would not have been too much of a leap. Unknown photographer.

This is another view of the same room showing the large floor-to-ceiling windows. Notice the copper luster pitcher placed in the center of the mantle. This could either be a true antique from the early nineteenth century or a copy made in the early twentieth to supply the demands of Colonial Revival decorators. The symmetry of the room, evident with the arrangement of objects and highlighted by the built-in bookcases was also a hallmark of this style. Unknown photographer.

The rocking chair on the left would have been described as "colonial" or perhaps to be more specific "Jacobean" in style. The thinness of the wood mixed with the designs from numerous style-centers of the eighteenth century confirm it as strictly a twentieth century piece. The small cabinet on the right is probably for sheet music or records. Unknown photographer.

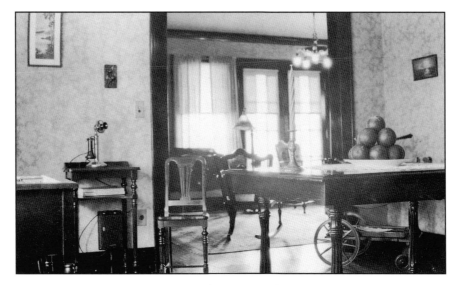

Looking from the dining room into the living room, there is one item that readily identified this as a twentieth century space. The candlestick telephone on the side table is clearly a modern feature. The furniture form of a telephone table is a modern appointment despite its early nineteenth century appearance. Unknown photographer.

The dining room furnishings carry on the Colonial, or to be specific, "Jacobean," style. Of particular interest is the glass-fronted china cabinet–a Victorian feature–now configured in a faintly eighteenth century style. One interesting item is the Mexican water bottle on top of the cabinet. Such items were popularized among large retail stores beginning in the late 1920's. The accompanying cup, however, is missing suggesting that it either broke or was put away so that the bottle could be used as a flower vase. Unknown photographer, circa 1920-30.

Chapter 6

The Arts and Crafts or a Mission in Life

The Arts and Crafts movement was not simply a style in the decorative arts but rather a widespread artistic, philosophic and architectural movement whose roots were in the seventeenth century Southwest, eighteenth century New England and nineteenth century Midwest. It was a movement that saw the evidence of handcraftsmanship as central to all work. Houses should have exposed beams and stonework with cut marks. Furniture should be without superficial ornament and with a corresponding emphasis on the natural wood or rattan. This was not only meant to show the honesty of the materials and construction but also the absence of the machine in the production process. This combination of ideas was critical to understanding the Arts and Crafts movement.

The Arts and Crafts style was truly an "art movement" unlike many other styles in that it had deep moral and philosophic overtones. The arrangement of objects, construction of furniture, and even curtains were part of the overall feeling of this movement. This snapshot, taken around 1910-20, highlights the artistic look of Arts and Crafts interiors during this time period. Unknown photographer.

Depending upon what part of the United States you lived in determined which particular manifestation of this movement appeared in your area. In the east, it was the seventeenth and eighteenth century simple furnishings of New England that inspired designers such as Elbert Hubbard and the Roycrofters or Gustav Stickley and the Craftsmen. Socialites, seeking opportunities for women, gave rise to potteries such as Rookwood in Ohio or the Saturday Night Girls in Boston. Houses decorated in this style often were sparsely furnished in stark contrast to late Victorian or Colonial Revival homes. When this style was first rediscovered during the 1970's, many saw the simple lines and sparseness as precursors of the streamlining of modern styling. Quite the contrary, the eastern Arts and Crafts movement had far more in common with the Colonial Revival–sans the clutter–than any other style. It saw the simplicity of the seventeenth century–with its use of joined oak–as the best way to decorate.

For those living in the west, it was the influence of the southwestern Indian culture fused with Mexican Latino culture that gave rise to the Mission style. The Mission style of the west often differed from that of Arts and Crafts in the east at a fundamental level. Whereas simplicity was often the rule in eastern interiors, western Mission houses often featured an abundance of decorative accessories–particularly Indian artifacts. A related set of influences came as a result of the opening of much of Latin America following the Mexican Revolution in the early part of the twentieth century. By the 1930's, department stores in the Midwest and east, along with those in the west, were selling Mexican pottery, rugs, and silver for a market fascinated with south of the border influences.

Two other variants of the style can be found in the bark furnishings of the Adirondacks and wicker or rattan furniture. Both types of furniture were representative of the Arts and Crafts view of using natural materials wherever possible. Adirondack furniture frequently used unprocessed birch limbs bound intricately together to create whimsical furniture suitable for cottages and bungalows. Wicker furniture, with its sinewy lines, is really a fusion of the Arts and Crafts with the Art Nouveau style. In fact, it could be argued that wicker furniture was the most successful interpretation by Americans of the Art Nouveau style. The Art Nouveau is usually thought to be predominantly a European movement with its origins grounded in the use of natural curvaceous designs as a response to the modern industrial world. Like the Arts and Crafts, it saw the machine-age as inherently evil with an earlier more natural world as being preferable. The use of natural fibers and the twisting curves found on most wicker furniture of this period suggests the strong influence of this style.

Arts and Crafts, Art Nouveau and even Colonial Revival can be broadly lumped together as styles that opposed the modern technological world manifested by late Victorian design. Interestingly, of the three styles, only the Colonial Revival really remained passed 1940. The Art Nouveau–never particularly popular in this country–really disappeared with the Depression. The Arts and Crafts style underwent several rebirths during the 1930's and 1940's. However by the end of the Second World War, it was gone until its rediscovery during the 1970's.

The Mission style of the Arts and Crafts movement was built around the Spanish styles of the southwest. The simple lines, bright colors and natural motifs of the interior of a Spanish Mission were often mirrored in the furnishings, architecture and arrangement of rooms. This photograph was taken by an amateur shutterbug in the 1920's. It shows the interior of a Spanish Mission in New Mexico. Notice the absence of benches for seating. The popular author Willa Cather wrote about seeing the Indians seated on brightly colored rugs while attending Mass in such a setting. Unknown photographer.

The Arts and Crafts movement was also heavily vested in decorating with American Indian art and artifacts. This remarkable interior features a number of southwestern and Great Plains Indian pieces including the painted buffalo hide, the blankets and the beaded parafleche. The furniture is identifiable through the incised orb as the trademark of the Roycroft Shops of East Aurora, New York. Founded by Elbert Hubbard, the Roycrofters were among the leading firms that produced Mission furniture and metal wares in the United States. Unknown photographer, circa 1910.

Rustic or twig furniture was another manifestation of the Arts and Crafts movement. These real photograph post cards are titled *Living Room* and *Fireplace*, both South Forks Inn, Buffalo, Wyo. and probably date from around 1910. The Indian rugs and Latino weavings are also typical features. The use of the stuffed animals would have been in keeping with the natural themes of the exposed logs and bark-covered furniture. Note the stuffed doe above the fireplace and the bird attached to the floor lamp. Unknown photographer.

This Mission style room, probably from the western United States, incorporates many of the furnishings that defined this particular style. The rectilinear armchair and table are typical of the work that could have been commissioned from great furniture makers like Gustav Stickley or purchased inexpensively from Sears Roebuck. The square lamp on the table would have had dark green glass. The Indian baskets and rugs along with the wicker bench were all hallmarks of this style. The only out of style piece is the built-in Gothic oak bench now covered with pillows and baskets. Unknown photographer, circa 1910.

Another room in this same house is equally furnished with a mixture of oak and wicker furniture. The cluttered arrangement of pictures on the walls as well as the openwork table runner would not have been acceptable to a "purist" decorator working in the Mission style. However, they do reflect many individual touches that soften the angular Mission furnishings.

The dining room of this same house continues the Mission styling with the square chairs and sideboard. Again, the strong visual display of china and glass harkens back to a Victorian aesthetic that was contrary to the pure Mission style interiors.

This view looks from the dining room back into the living room. Notice the wicker tea cart in the corner. Wicker, like fumed oak, was the most popular of materials in an Arts and Crafts interior.

This image is believed to date from 1906 and shows the dining room of a home in San Francisco. The use of so many built-in features and cabinets was typical of bungalow architecture in Mission style homes. Notice the exposed brickwork–a feature common to bungalows–that emphasized the hand-built aspects of the building. Unknown photographer.

These photographs were removed from a photo album belonging to a friend of the author. The young man in the far right of both is the author's grandfather visiting his aunt and uncle at a house near Pittsburgh around 1910. Notice the spade motifs incorporated into the decoration of both rooms. These clues, like the wicker chair, are further evidence of the Arts and Crafts taste. Unknown photographer.

The Arts and Crafts style could be mixed with many different furnishings without losing the feel of the movement. The furnishings in this room are a mixture of sophisticated Mission pieces such as the desk and corner cabinet along with a Colonial Revival mantle and Victorian gas fixture and clock. The oriental or floral pattern carpet would also have been more in keeping with Victorian or Colonial Revival tastes rather the sandy colors of the Arts and Crafts. The use of the Indian baskets and the abundance of plants are more in keeping with the Arts and Crafts tastes. Unknown photographer, circa 1910.

Another room setting that mixes various styles including the Arts and Crafts as well as the Colonial Revival. The wicker chair and oak table are typical Mission furnishings while the copper teapot and Queen Anne revival chair are Colonial Revival. Unknown photographer, circa 1930.

These three images show a typical home of about 1920 or so. The styles represent the Colonial Revival (the mantle and reproduction Empire-style bureau), Arts and Crafts (the wicker chair, library table and Indian art print) as well as the older Victorian (the Moorish table lamp that would have been popular in the 1880's). Again, mixing styles and periods was common then, as today, in that it showed the ranging tastes of the owner. Unknown photographer, circa 1920.

The ultimate incorporation of nearly fifty years in decorating styles can be found in this photograph of a bungalow from New York State. The Mission hanging lamp in the dining room along with the wicker rocker are the basic Arts and Crafts elements in the room. There is also a strong smattering of reproduction colonial furnishings including the piano stool and center table–all of which were made around 1910 or so. Then there is a large group of late Victorian pieces including the Eastlake side chair in the background and the ceramic figure on the piano. The floral carpeting and doilies are also indicative of late nineteenth century design and tastes. Unknown photographer, circa 1910.

While photography can be argued to be the greatest change for the decorative arts during the late nineteenth century, the arrival of the horseless carriage in mainstream American towns surely must have been the most striking.

Such a change did not occur overnight as the photographs on the following pages document the slow progression from horse-drawn to gas-powered vehicles. No better example of this change can be seen in the street-cars that utilized a combination of electric power and horses. Never completely reliant on the new technology of electricity and motors, horses remained an important form of transportation into the early twentieth century. The relationship between man and horse had existed for millennia. As these images show, the pride that we manifest today in our SUV's or roadsters can be seen in the well-groomed horses and shiny carriages of the late nineteenth century.

It is interesting to note the attire of the two gentlemen who are shown out for an afternoon in this road wagon. The carriage is primarily designed for speed and it is likely that they are out for a pleasure run. Unknown photographer, circa 1890.

And like the cars of today, there were tremendous variations in carriage body types and luxury amenities. Simple gigs were available for those who wanted sporty and fast while luxury surreys could be obtained for taking the family out for a picnic. In between were the multipurpose vehicles such as road wagons that could be used for both genteel families as well as sport-minded individuals. In your luxury carriage, there could be brackets to hold cut glass vases for flowers that would be mounted above a velvet lined liquor chest.

The Columbus Carriage and Harness Company of Columbus, Ohio published a one hundred thirty-eight page catalog of which seventy-nine pages were reserved for different carriages. Surprisingly, the difference in price between a low-end runabout and a high-end surrey was only about twenty-five dollars. What is unstated is that

the ownership of any wooden carriage also presumed a house with a carriage shed behind–a luxury that few people had. The result was that livery and drover services were more prevalent than taxis of today.

With the rise of the automobile, the electric street car and other modern forms of conveyance, cities faced another new aspect of modernity–the traffic jam. While runaway horses were serious issues in the nineteenth century, they had nothing on the risks involved in automotive accidents and traffic congestion. As you look at these images, imagine the silence that must have existed without automotive traffic. At the same time, imagine the pungent smell of horses and the sense of time that was needed to travel even short distances. Perhaps the horseless carriage–while not as romantic as being out for a runabout–was infinitely more practical.

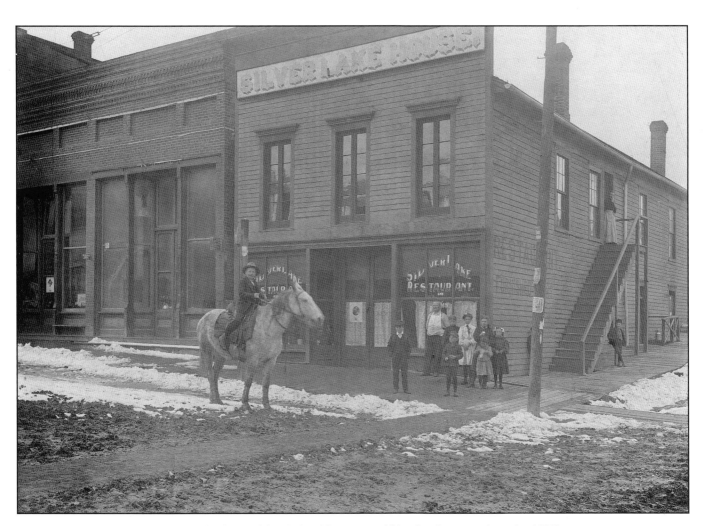

This photograph taken in Silver Lakes Montana could be dated anytime from the 1880's to the 1920's. Horses were an important, and in many cases, the only form of transportation for much of America well into the twentieth century. Notice the dirt street with the packed earth or wooden sidewalks. The Hotel and restaurant on the corner has a typical false storefront as did many businesses during this period. Unknown photographer, circa 1900.

Riding horses for pleasure continues to this day. These images, taken near Washington, DC, date from around 1930. Unknown photographer, images taken from original glass plate negatives.

This young lad is out for a run-about in his horse drawn gig. The gig was among the popular of recreational carriages used in nineteenth century America. The photo is titled *Elsie and Harry, 1898* although we are not sure if this refers to the boy, girl or horse. Unknown photographer.

Today we think of only adults as driving cars or carriages but evidence from several of these images suggests that children were trained to drive at an early age. This young girl appears to be taking the family road wagon out for a spin. Unknown photographer, circa 1890.

This is the famed surrey with the "fringe on top" of fame in the Broadway musical *Oklahoma*. Here a family is out for a drive in a photo titled *The Team at Spot Pond–Stoneham Mass. June 18, 1895*. Unknown photographer.

In contrast to the family out for a drive in the country, here are two working men–probably farmers–out in their carriage. This early tintype shows a leather harness on the horse to keep flies from settling. The scene is probably from south central Pennsylvania. Unknown photographer, circa 1870.

This south central Pennsylvania (the clue being the large bank barn on the hill) scene shows an elderly man on his road wagon. This photo differs from the earlier example in that he has it hooked up to a team rather than a single horse. It is possible that he is taking the group out for a Sunday spin in the country. Unknown photographer, circa 1890.

Not all horse drawn vehicles were for pleasure. Delivery wagons were an important feature of everyday life. Here a milk wagon is making a delivery to a large public building–possibly a school. Unknown photographer, probably from the Midwest, circa 1900.

Ole Mule Car, Mode of Rapid Transit in Vogue in El Paso from 1885 to1901.
Unknown photographer.

One man safety car with two multi-plow internal combustion motors, capable of high starting effort. Winchester, Kentucky, 1903. Unknown photographer.

Central Park, New York City, circa 1900.
Unknown photographer.

International Railway Company, Buffalo, NY. Unknown photographer, circa 1910.

This is an early electric streetcar that marries the form of the older horse-drawn car with the new technology. Unknown photographer, circa 1915.

Chapter 8
Relaxation and Leisure

Modern concepts of leisure are a phenomena of the twentieth century. For the affluent, vacations and leisure often meant extended travel away from home. For the poor, there simply was no concept of such breaks from a world where work was a seven-day a week occurrence. For the middle class, however, leisure was a new phenomenon that came to be embraced in a huge way. As the work week grew smaller and incomes increased, the idea of travel to exotic locations became particularly appealing. If your budget could not afford Peru then the Corn Palace in Sioux City might be more manageable. And to record the event, you had to bring your new camera. The new hobby of photography fed into this wanderlust and thus we have tremendous numbers of images recording Americans at play.

The *Corn Palace* in Sioux City, Iowa, was one of the many regional attractions that brought both rural and urban visitors together. With patriotic and religious motifs, the Corn Palace—as seen by the crowds in the foreground—was the perfect "wholesome" family attraction. Marked "Genelli, Corn Palace Views, 1890. Sioux City, Ia."

The two photographs that begin this chapter illustrate this point from the perspective of photography. The first is of a single man and the second of a large family, both having the common element of being taken outdoors. Although staged rather than impromptu, such a scene–thanks to technological advancements in photography–was possible, and popular, during this period. The deeper question is "why outdoors?" One answer might be that the rise of the modern world in the late nineteenth century prompted families to seek out nature as an alternative to smoky and dark rooms.

Swimming, hunting, fishing and winter hobbies were among the many outdoor activities available during this period. Notice in all of the images how gender roles are defined. Fishing was not exclusively a male pastime as the images show an equal balance between the sexes. Hunting, on the other hand, was an almost exclusively male hobby. Winter hobbies such as sleigh riding were reserved for families or children regardless of gender. While such gender definitions are limited by the evidence that we have, these conclusions even seem logical today.

Gardening also becomes an important hobby for many Americans during this time period. In prior years, only the rich could afford to hire gardeners to tend to the difficult tasks associated with cultivating plants at home. With the rising popularity of gardening among the middle class, garden shops and books on the subject were more readily available. The popularity of recreational gardening can really be traced to the opening of public garden spaces in the years around the Civil War. The rise of the modern public cemetery movement begins then with an emphasis on the garden and park aspects rather than rows of tombstones. Images from large public parks in the east, such as Central Park in New York or the Public Gardens in Boston were popular in Victorian parlors. Not only did they bring a little bit of nature into the home but they served as inspirations for local "green thumbs."

Plants in the house were another sign of changing views. To be able to spend time raising plants indoors was seen as a suitably genteel activity for a proper lady. The very richest in America had gardeners who focused upon keeping their properties well tended. For the aspiring and newly affluent middle class, however, flower gardens were a sign of affluence as well–albeit with a different spin. Well-manicured gardens or abundant houseplants were a sign that the family had sufficient wealth to afford cleaning help so that leisure time could be devoted to plants. The result was the widespread popularity of the bay window conservatory, the multi-tiered plant stand and the popular cultivation of difficult ornamentals like roses. A blooming plant came to represent the mark of a successful homemaker.

The other great new hobby of the time was travel. Unlike today when people will cover hundreds of miles visiting many different destinations in a single trip, Victorians usually pursued only limited stops. Seaside resorts such as Atlantic City were founded in the third quarter of the nineteenth century to provide recreation for eastern seaboard city dwellers. Inland in the east, the Chautauqua movement introduced families to camp meeting life around lakes and mountains. Initially begun under religious camp meeting auspices, Chautauquas became far more secular over the succeeding decades. In south central Pennsylvania, Mt. Gretna was such a spot. It still exists as a summer getaway for families from the nearly cities of Lancaster, Harrisburg and Philadelphia.

Recreation for those who were not interested in the great outdoors could also be found in civil, religious and fraternal societies. Musicales and lyceums provided opportunities for the more literary minded. Fraternal organizations with their elaborate rituals and regalia were another source of relaxation for much of society. Upper middle class men joined the Freemasons while others, perhaps with less deep pocket books, settled for any one of the host of copycat groups that existed.

Ironically, the popularity of gardening and travel as recreation is still relevant today while most of the nineteenth century secret, fraternal and related civic societies are rapidly disappearing. At the end of the nineteenth century, no politician could expect to be elected to office without numerous titles and affiliations after his name. Today, it would be difficult to find anyone who belongs to more than one or two such organizations–if that many at all. Perhaps this can be explained by the general acceptance of "family recreation." Uni-sex organizations, while occasionally inviting spouses or families to participate, were by their nature closed and restricted. The result is that these groups have nearly all disappeared in favor of the more popular family activities.

Outdoor photography had been practiced many years before it was brought into the realm of formal portraiture. This anonymous young man was photographed outdoors standing by a rocker draped in a paisley shawl. Such casual scenes were a dramatic departure from the earlier and more formal studio images taken a decade earlier. Unknown photographer, circa 1880-90.

Family outdoor photographs are even more rare than individual portraits. This family–decked out in their Sunday best–brought a little bit of their parlor into the great outdoors. The patent furniture rockers, lamp and books were all probably dragged from the formal parlor outside and posed in front of a grape arbor to create this rather incongruous scene. Unknown photographer, circa 1898.

Going on an outing into the great outdoors was then, like today, a popular pastime. Here a group of young people, their traveling wagon parked behind, are shown sitting on the grass enjoying a picnic. The obvious mixed company (including the shocking scene of a young man resting his head on the woman's lap in the foreground) would not have appeared in a photograph taken a decade earlier. Unknown photographer, circa 1900.

Bicycle riding was another huge nineteenth century phenomena. This scene, probably taken at either the Pennsylvania Chatauqua or Camp Meeting at Mt. Gretna, shows a man and woman posed in front of their small cabin with a rather sporty bicycle sitting out in front. Perhaps he has come to call upon her in his new bike and the image was captured by an anonymous photographer in this circa 1890 photograph.

Winter fun had a particular appeal to children as this photograph of a young sled rider and a pony reveals. Notice the small coach or horse whip held by the girl although it appears to be rather ineffective in getting the animal moving. The image is titled on the reverse *Dorothy has someone to pull her*. Unknown photographer, circa 1910.

Outdoor activities such as camping and fishing were another popular pursuit. Here are group of well-dressed woodsmen assembling their fishing gear before heading out to the lake or stream. Unknown photographer, circa 1890.

Fly fishing, often thought until recently to be a "man's sport," was clearly practiced by both sexes. Here, two well-dressed women are shown with their husbands or guides positioned on rocks while fishing. Marked "Hammond's Studio, Porterville, Calif.", circa 1910.

Above and opposing page:
These three images are from a photo scrapbook kept by the author's great uncle, Albert Leander Swift, and depict a fishing trip to Canada around 1900. Notice that the guide is charged with cooking the meal along with rowing the boat and holding the fish. The lady is Ella B. Thompson Swift. Unknown photographer–possibly Albert L. Swift, circa 1900.

Another unusual outdoor pursuit was astronomy. These images were made from original glass plate negatives taken by an amateur shutterbug. They show the types of home telescopes that could be purchased or made in order to study the stars. Unknown photographer, circa 1930.

Titled *General View Public Garden, Boston Mass and Vicinity,* this image contains a wealth of detail about how public gardens were laid out and used. Today, we often think of huge displays of flowers and plants as necessary for public gardens. In looking at this photograph, sparseness seems to be the rule. There is a mix of flower beds interspersed with potted exotics. The palm trees, in particular, would not have survived the cold of Boston outdoors but would have been wintered over in a conservatory. Notice as well that the gardeners have laid boards out on the planted beds in order to work in the center of the garden without damaging existing plantings. Marked on the reverse Moulton-Erickson Photograph Co., Salem Mass., circa 1890.

The wide path, bench and "natural" (probably man-made) bridge are all indicative of a public garden space. Interestingly, unlike the formal garden shown in Boston, this area was conceived as a natural garden with ferns and pines as landscape features. In the late nineteenth century, public gardens became the rage as places to escape the dirt and grime of city life. Titled *At Hunnewells, June 6, 1891*, unknown photographer, dated 1891.

Titled *Washington, Rear Pall Ave. Bldg.* this is probably a scene from a large private property in our nation's capital. The reflecting pool and statuary reflect formal Italian garden design. Unknown photographer, circa 1930, from an original glass plate negative.

This garden is on the grounds of the Masonic Homes in Elizabethtown, Lancaster County, Pennsylvania. While private property, these grounds are open–even to this day–to the general public. The Italian pergola or walkway is the most striking feature of this formal garden. Roses, daylilies and evergreens define the internal spaces while an arboreal border is the outer boundary. Unknown photographer, circa 1930.

One of the best spots for a public garden was on the grounds of state capitol buildings as can be seen in this photograph from the Pennsylvania capitol complex at Harrisburg. Here, a decorative fountain is flanked by pots of calendula and ferns. The grounds were, and still are, populated by squirrels imported to the city by a governor who wanted to add a little wildlife to the capitol! Unknown photographer., circa 1890.

Another public-private garden was the conservatory for the White House in Washington, DC. With its abundant plantings, this formal greenhouse was a place for the public–as well as the President–to visit and escape the noise of the city. Marked "Sold by Underwood and Underwood, Baltimore, Md., Ottawa, Kas." Circa 1880.

Having plants indoors was not seen just as a decorative touch but also as a manifestation of the talents of the housewife in being able to tend and keep beautiful plants. In this parlor, there are a wide range of plant materials including Boston and Asparagus ferns, a Wandering Jew, and some type of flowering plant located on the window sill. The flair for the exotic can also be seen in the conch shell located on the center table. Unknown photographer, circa 1900.

This parlor was probably located somewhere in the southern United States because of the gauzy curtains and louvered window shutters. The double pair of luxuriant Boston ferns visually sets the entire room into a near perfect symmetry. Unknown photographer, circa 1900.

The late nineteenth century was a period when exotic travel began to become popular albeit among either the rich or as a missionary. Shown here is a gentleman with a collection of exotic items that her perhaps brought back from a trip to the Orient. The scene is staged in a commercial photographer's studio although undoubtedly the props belonged to the subject. Marked "Goodman, Whitewater Wis." Circa 1900.

Swimming was another popular past time in this period. Atlantic City–where this photograph was taken around 1912–was the first of many such beach resorts. Albert L. Swift (right) and his nephew Harley L. Swift, are shown on the beach with a rescue boat in the background. Unknown photographer (possibly Ella B. Thompson Swift), circa 1912.

Left:
Many of the earliest tourist destinations were places that still remain popular to this day. Washington, D.C., the Gettysburg Battlefield, Valley Forge and the Statue of Liberty were early tourist destinations for middle class tourists looking for a spot to spend a summer holiday. This early automotive touring coach from Washington, D.C., was based upon a horse drawn nineteenth century roof-seat break. Notice the wide range of attire. One wonders if it was possible to see past the lady's hat in the fourth row. Unknown photographer. Dated July 9, 1908.

The Chautauqua Movement was one of the most popular summer activities of the late nineteenth and early twentieth centuries. Founded at New York's Lake Chautauqua, these religious summer camps–later secularized and made into middle class retreats–spread throughout the eastern United States. This shows the front porch of the Brunner Cottage at Mt. Gretna, Lebanon County, Pennsylvania around 1912. The large Chinese lanterns were typical of front porch decorations that were used then–and still are to this day–at many of the Chautauquas. Unknown photographer, circa 1912.

Summer cottages could go beyond the simple three-room Chautauqua cabin to the large seaside house. Here is an elaborate home built at Nantasket Beach, Massachusetts. In the shingle Victorian style, it featured probably about a dozen rooms including the cupola on top. The young trees are a clue that this was a recently developed area rather than an older established resort where the plantings had grown much larger. Unknown photographer, circa 1890.

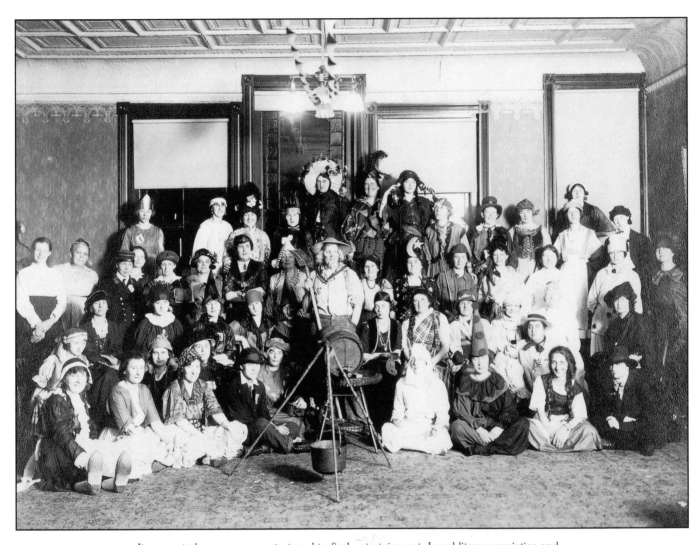

It was not always necessary to travel to find entertainment. Local literary societies and thespian groups also provided outlets for folks in the pre-television and radio era. Here a group of amateur performers are shown decked out in their costumes. Although we don't know if it was for a play, variety show or gala, it was a unisex event with no men evident anywhere in the photograph. Unknown photographer, dated 1920.

Fraternal organizations were another outlet for both men and women in this period. Shown here is a man dressed in the regalia of either a Masonic Knights Templar or a Knight of the Golden Eagle. These organizations, with their elaborate rituals and militaristic attire, were popular middle class past times. Marked "Bonebrake, 907½ Main Street, Terre Haute, Ind." Circa 1890.

Men's only clubs and fraternal organizations were popular outlets around the turn of the century. Although this appears to be a rather typical late nineteenth century parlor, the photographs of men along the wall (probably past Presidents) and the abundance of spittoons on the floor, point to the use of the space as a clubroom. The furniture, described as Eastlake in style, was purchased en-suite for use in such a room. Notice the absence of small items also suggesting the public use of this room. Unknown photographer, circa 1880.

Chapter 9

Technology Changes Everything

Technology was changing rapidly during the late nineteenth and early twentieth centuries. This scene–although unidentified–could have been photographed anywhere in the United States during this period. The record player was the first step in a series of important changes that dramatically affected domestic life. From radio to the television and then the video game, all of these devices ultimately spelled the death knell for the multitude of fraternal organizations, musicales and other activities of the late nineteenth century. Unknown photographer, circa 1915.

The popularization of the automobile also changed domestic life. Families were far more mobile than they ever had been as the abundance and reliability of cars touched nearly everyone. Fifty years before this photograph was taken, the same scene could have been created with a horse and carriage in front of the house. Unknown photographer, circa 1920-30.

As the automobile became more popular, so Americans became used to that other modern phenomena–the traffic jam. This scene, from an unknown downtown, shows the urban issues of traffic congestion for not only cars but also electric streetcars and the hazards of being a pedestrian. The two traffic policemen in the center of this photograph have a formidable task ahead of them in controlling this situation. Unknown photographer, circa 1920-30.

Right:
As this book began with formal studio photography, so it will end with this image of a mother and child. While the mother was instructed not to look at the camera, such a command was not understood by the infant who is busy studying the situation. This formalized portrait of maternal love and domestic harmony differs tremendously from the early interior views and studio portraits. Gone is the strip carpeting in favor of area rugs. Clean tables, modern electric lamps and shiny brass beds are the most striking features of this room. These spaces are no longer about style and taste but rather they are a direct reflection of America's obsession with cleanliness. Rooms must be brighter than bright, cleaner than clean. The result is an emphasis on colors, fabrics and materials that are high in maintenance and thus noteworthy to the outsider as symbols of hard work and cleanliness. Unknown photographer, circa 1930.

These two prints–taken from original glass plate negatives– show street scenes in New York City around 1930. The skyscraper is the dominant feature of the landscape and inspired Upton Sinclair to write about *The Urban Jungle*. Such changes had begun occurring during the late nineteenth century but it was not until the 1930's that as a nation we had come to celebrate the skyscraper as the ultimate symbol of the modern world. Unknown photographer from original glass plate negatives.

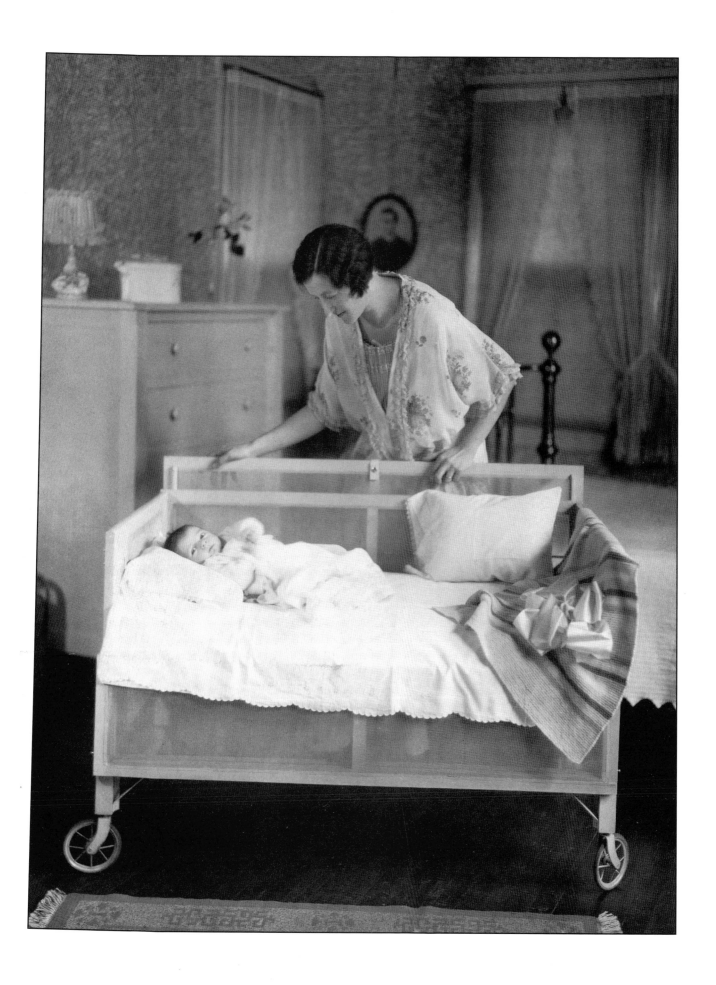

Bibliography

Bettmann, Otto L. *The Good Old Days–They Were Terrible.* New York: Random House, 1974.

Bowman, Leslie Green. *American Arts and Crafts: Virtue in Design.* Boston: Bulfinch Press, 1991.

Bryon, Joseph. *New York Interiors at the Turn* 1976.

Calloway, Stephen and Elizabeth Cromley. *The Interior Architectural Details.* New York: Sim

Foy, Jessica and Karal Ann Marling. *The Arts an* University of Tenn. Press, 1994.

Garrett, Wendell, et al. *The Arts in America:* Scribner's Sons, 1969.

Haslam, Malcolm. *In the Nouveau Style.* New Y

Henisch, H.K. and B.A. *The Photograph Experi* Press, 1988.

Lind, Carla. *The Wright Style.* New York: Simon

Maass, Johnny. *The Gingerbread Age: A View* House, 1983.

Seale, William. *The Tasteful Interlude: America 1917.* Nashville: American Association for S

Seale, William. *Recreating the Historic House Int* and Local History, 1979.

Shaw, Simon. *Frontier House.* New York: Atria

Tracy, Berry and Marilynn Johnson. *19th-Centu Arts.* New York: New York Graphic Society,

Winter, Robert and Alexander Vertikoff. *Amer* Schuster, 1996.